Life in Greek Mythology

Coloring Book

Volume 2

✓ **50 coloring pages**
✓ **Ideal for colored pencils, markers or pencils**
✓ **Large print page format: 8.5 x 11 inches**
✓ **Single-sided pages to avoid leaks. Making sure your masterpieces stay clean!**

Copyright © 2024 by Al&Vy
All rights reserved

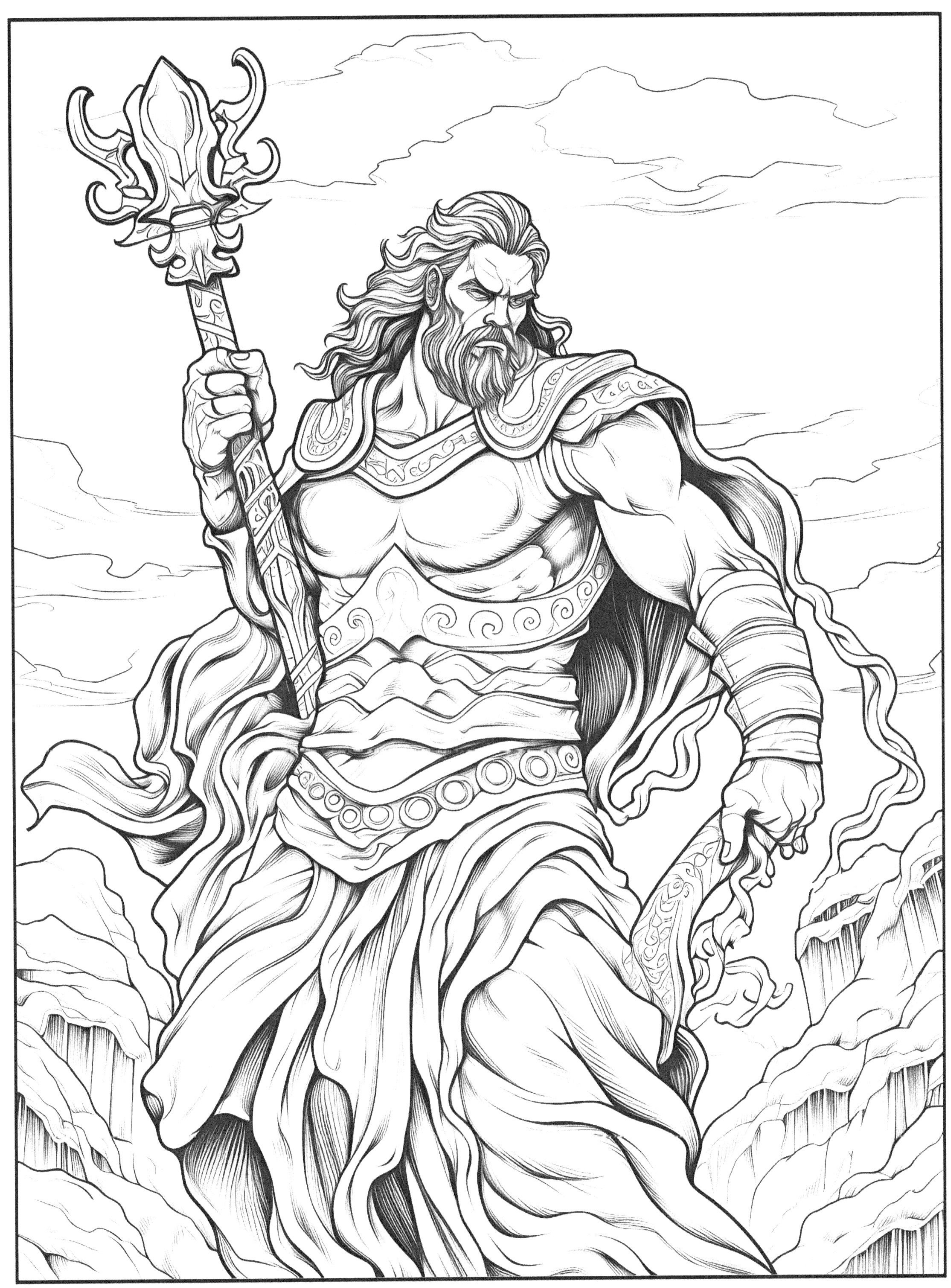

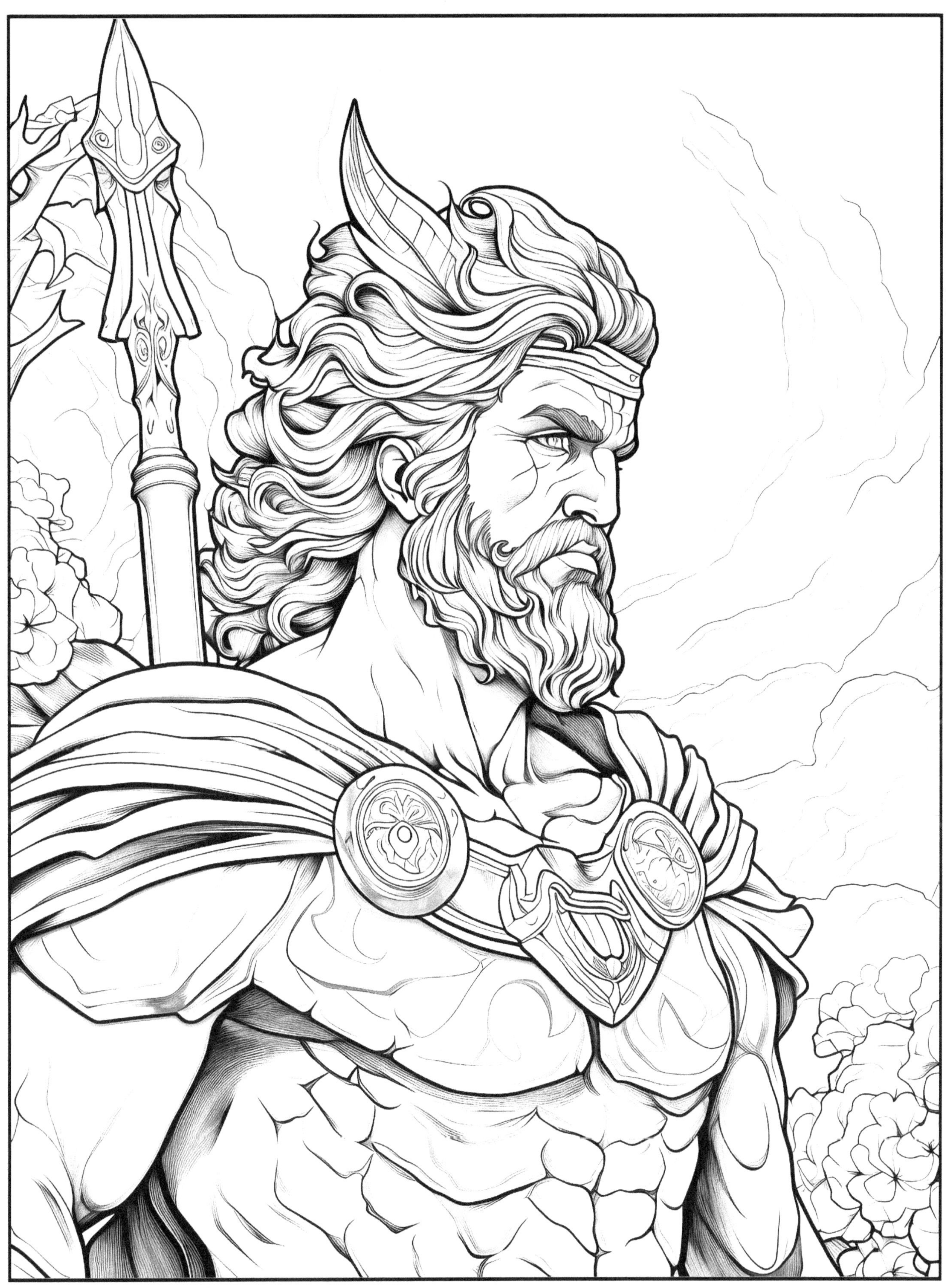

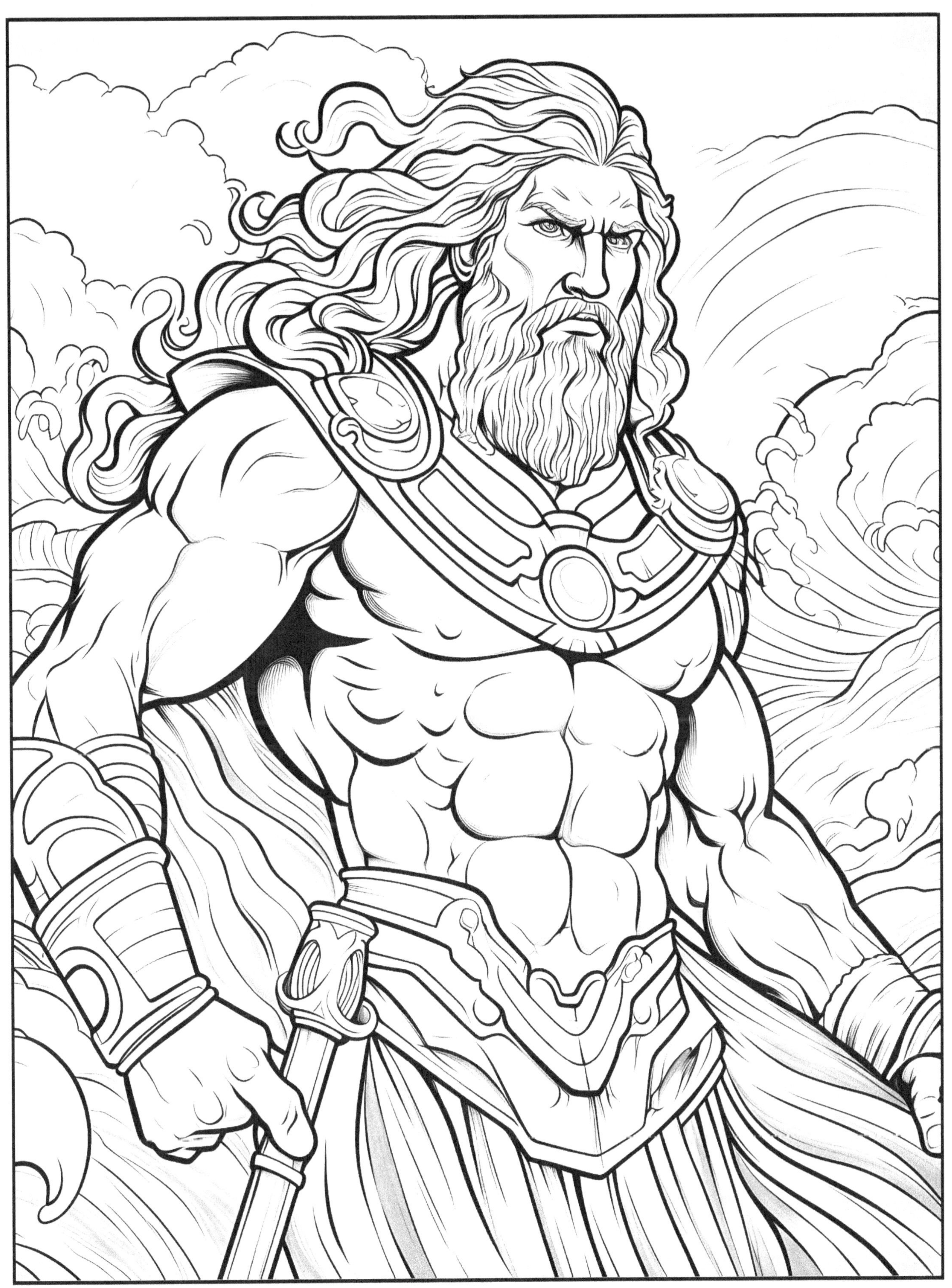

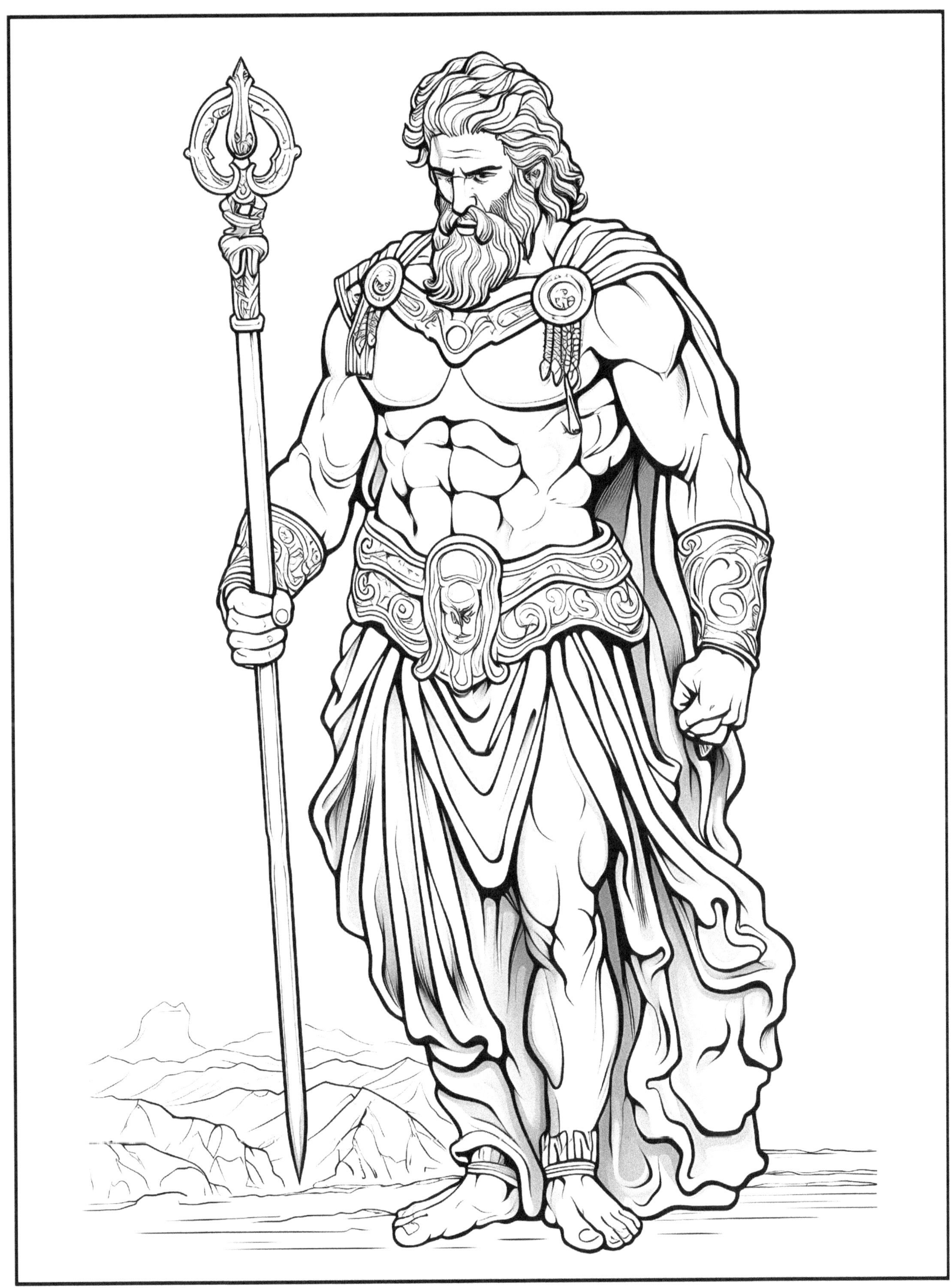

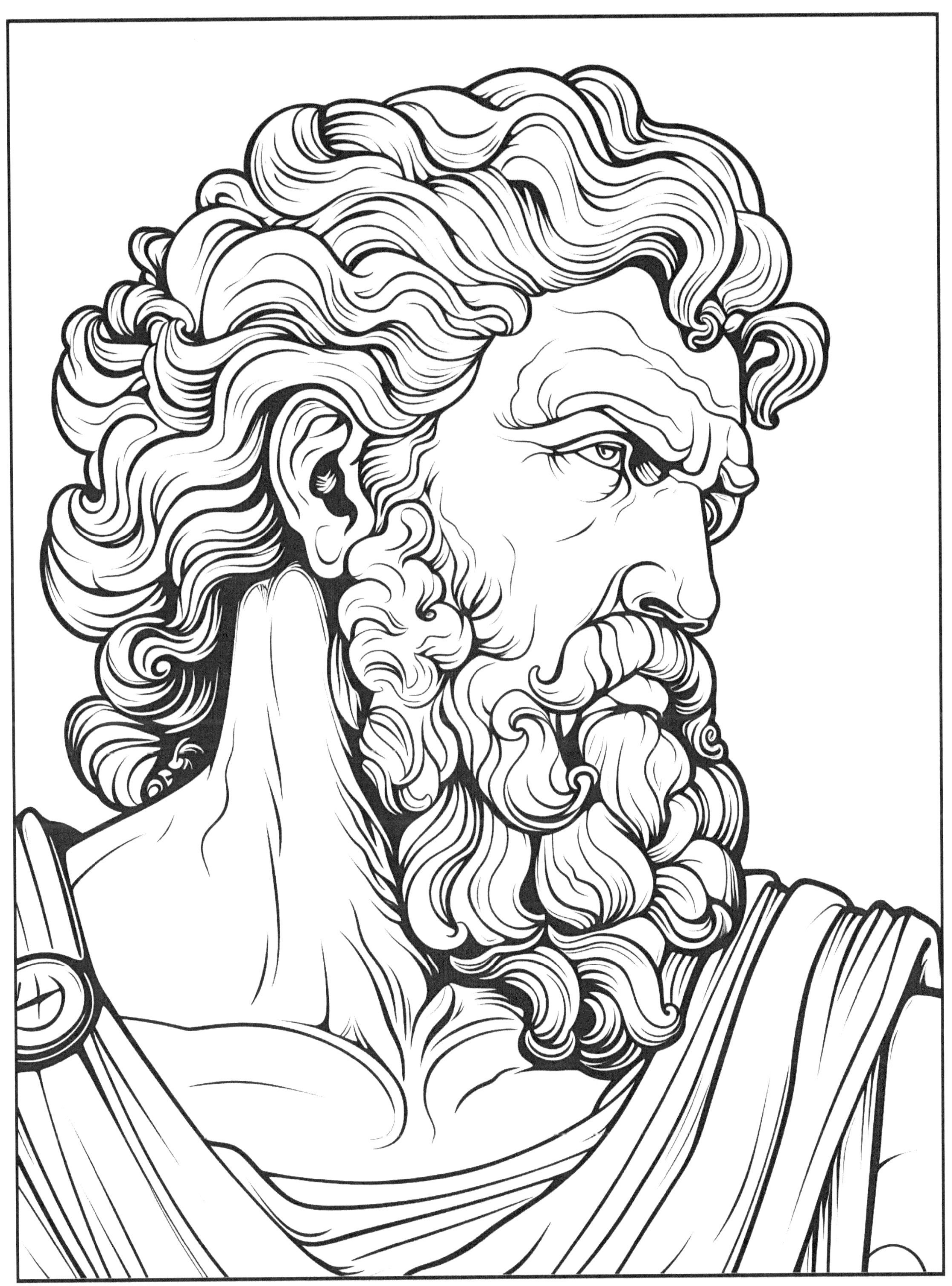

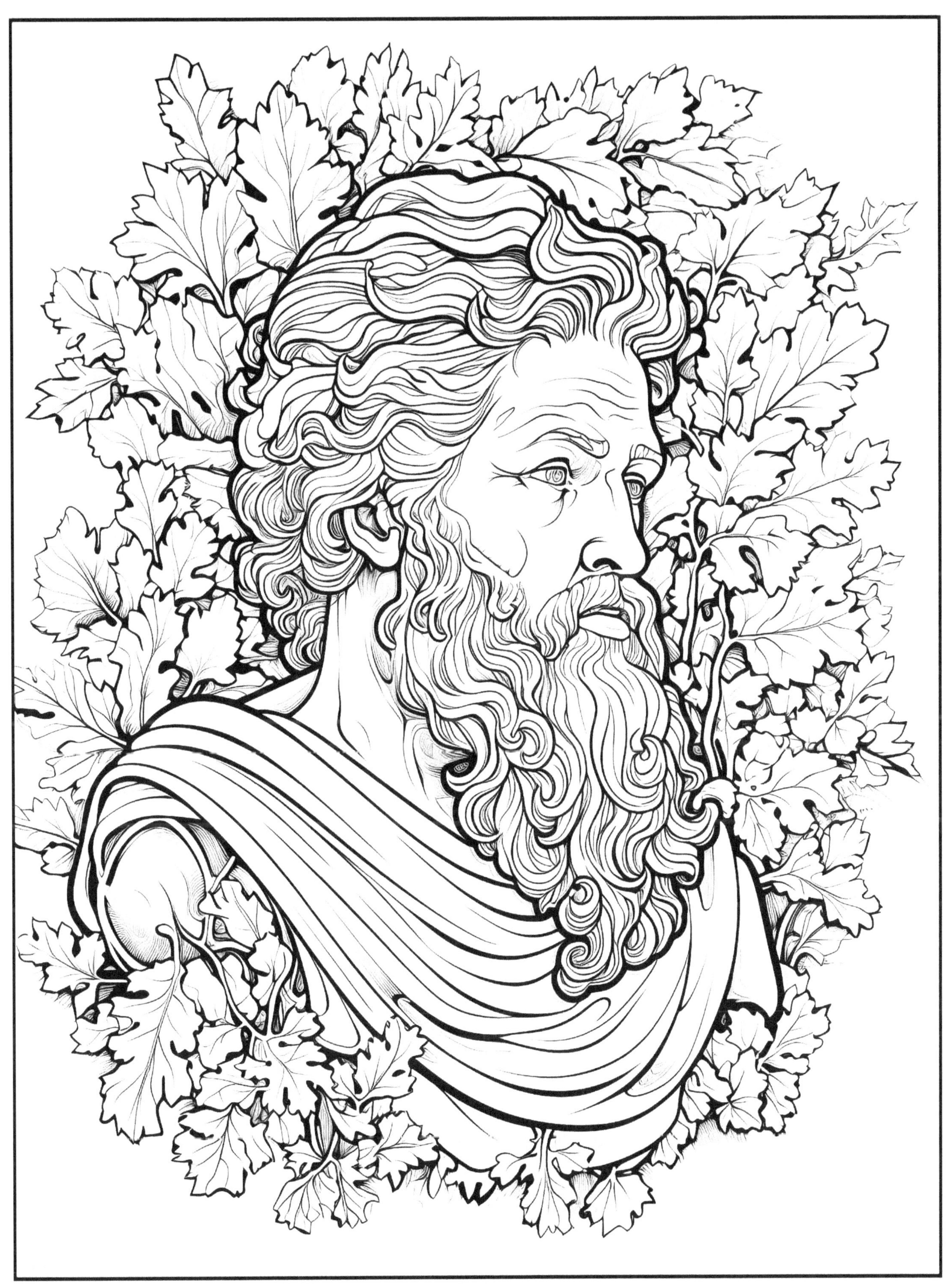

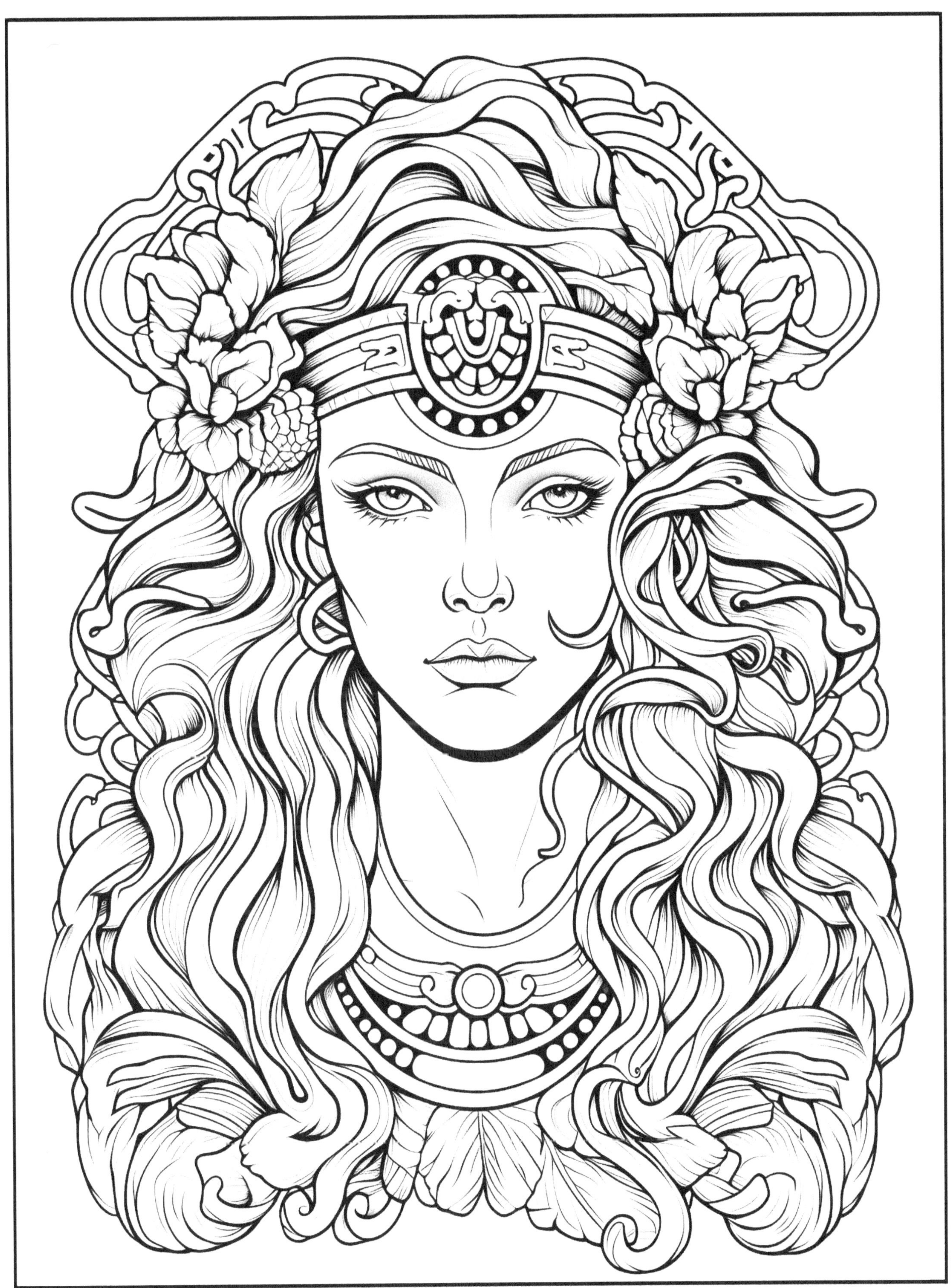

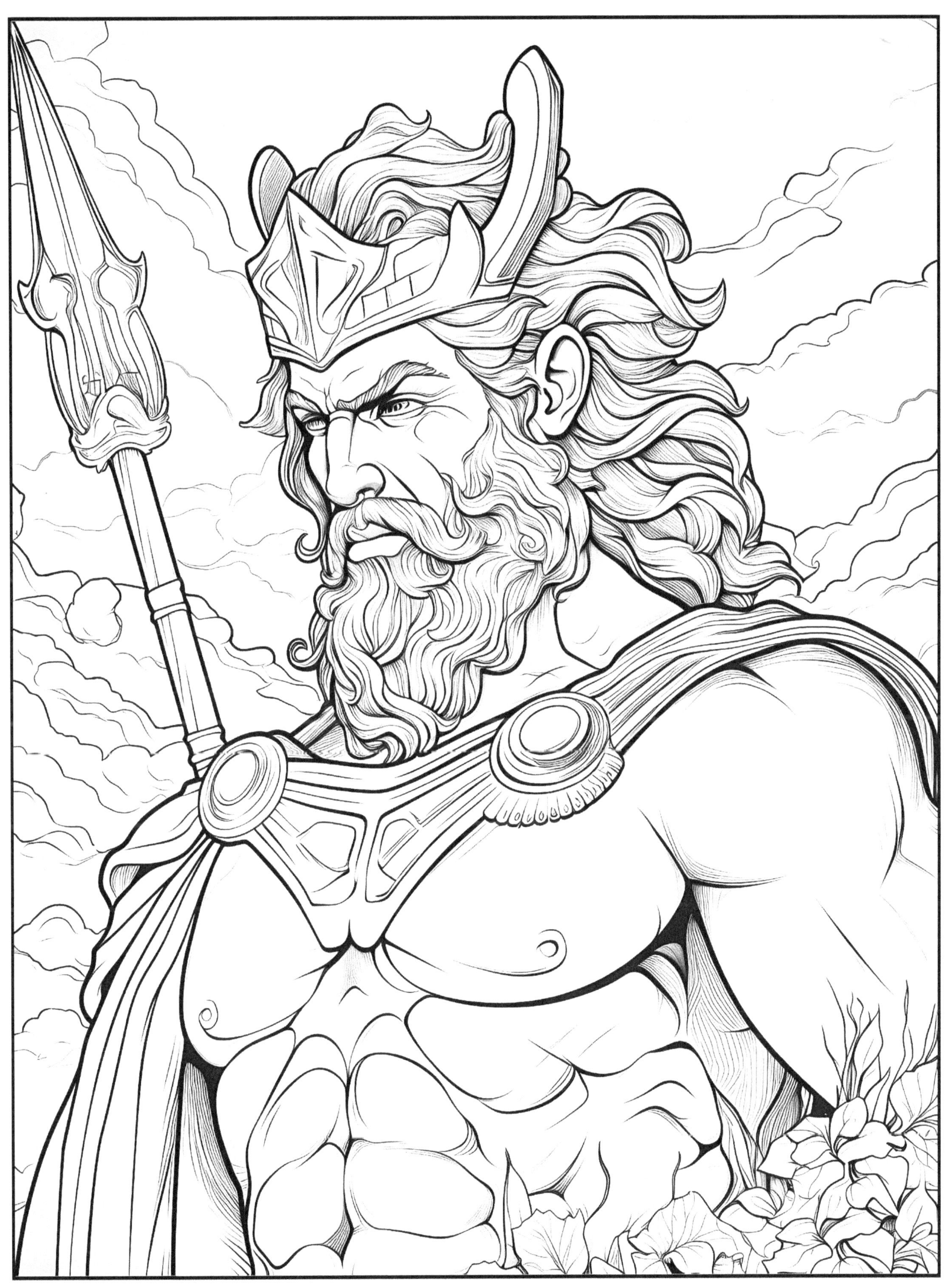

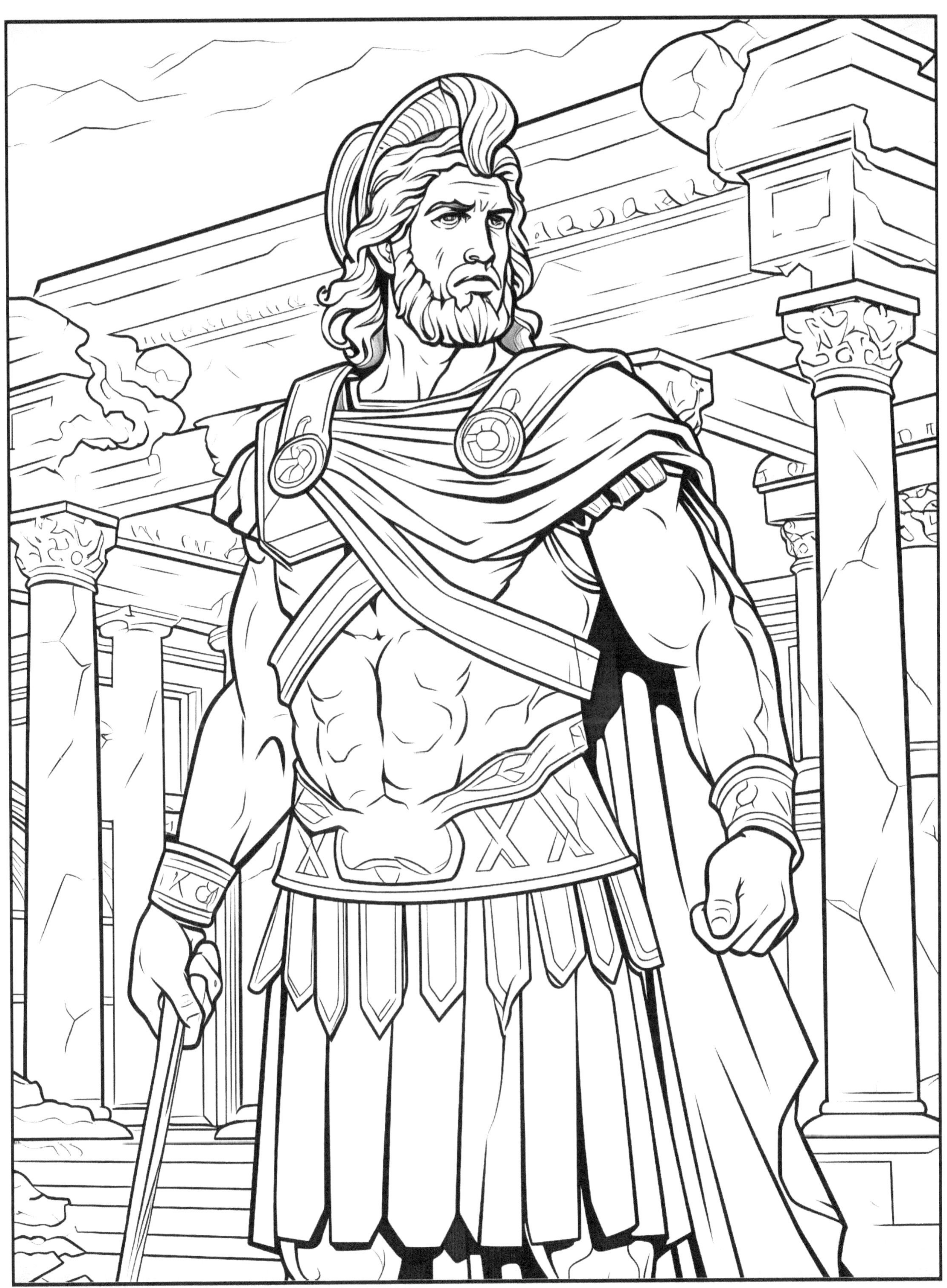

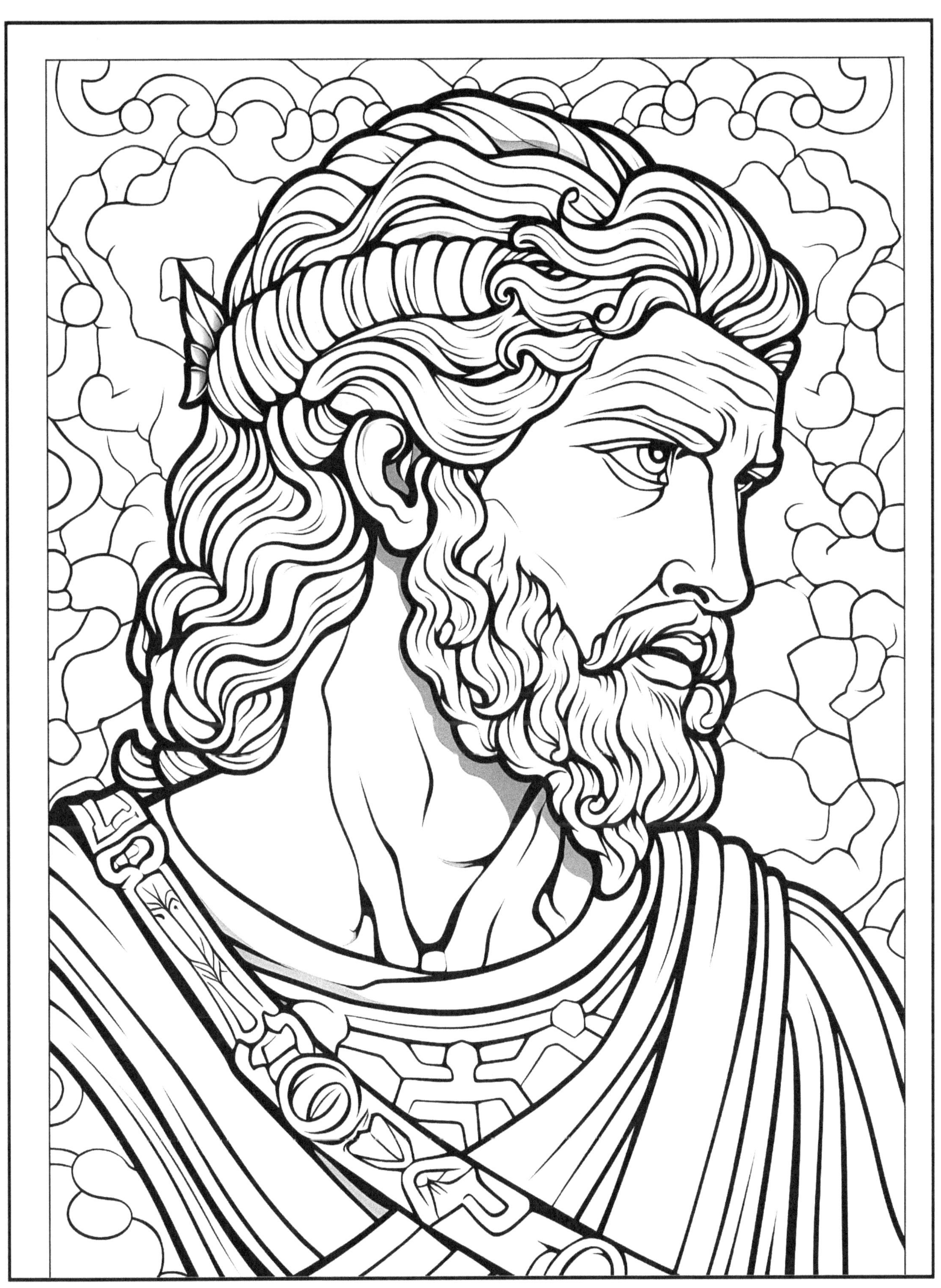

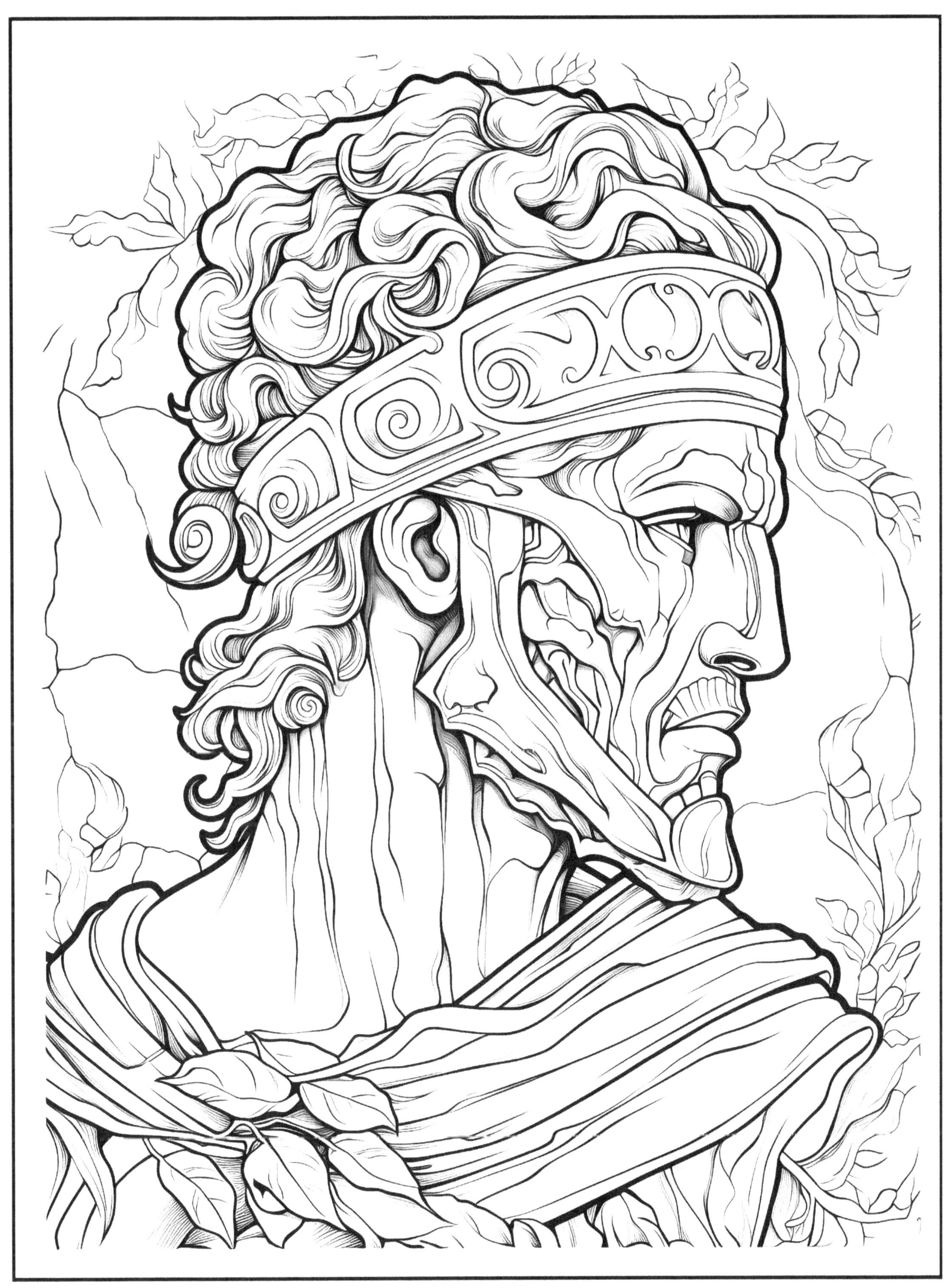

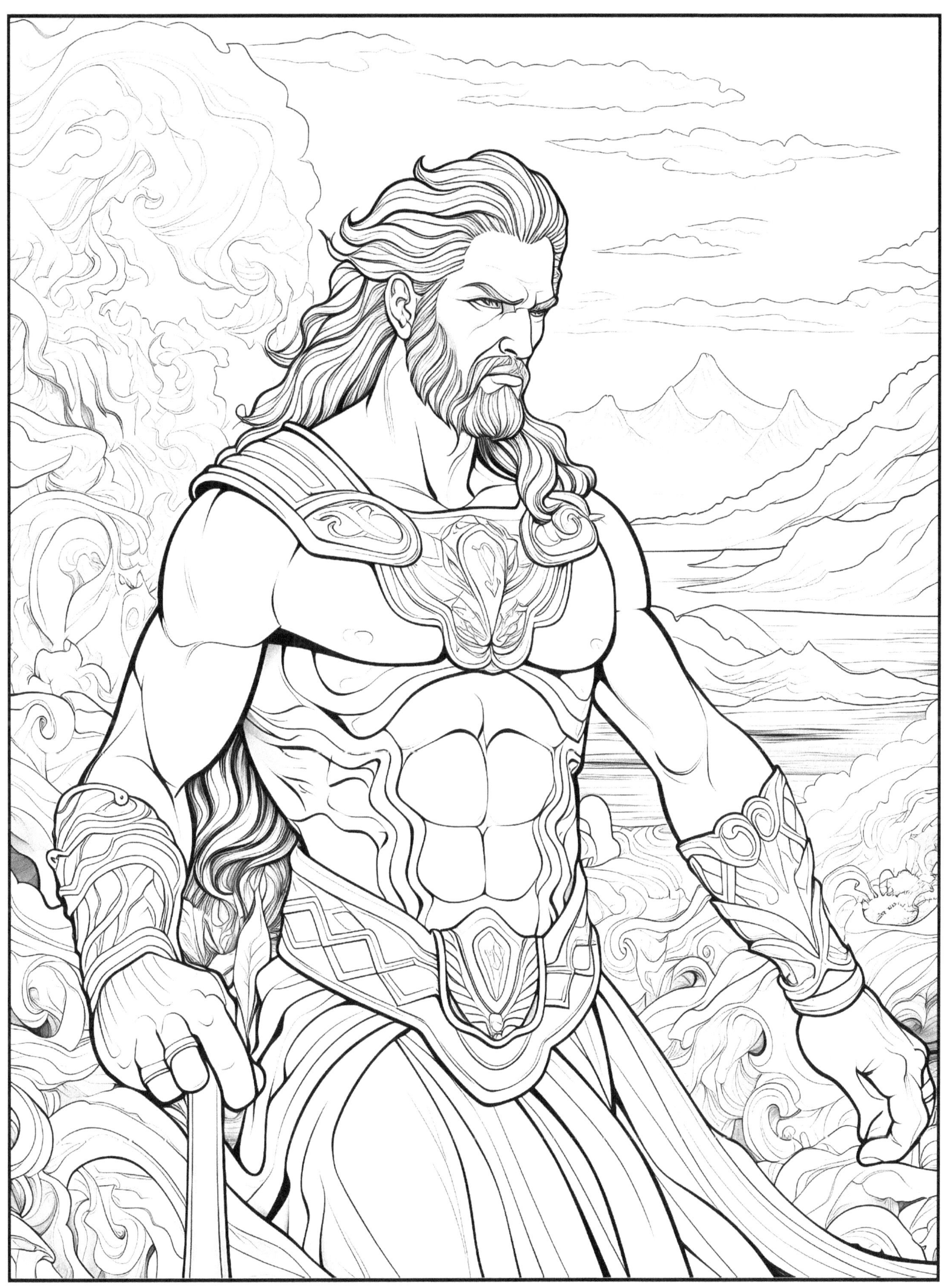

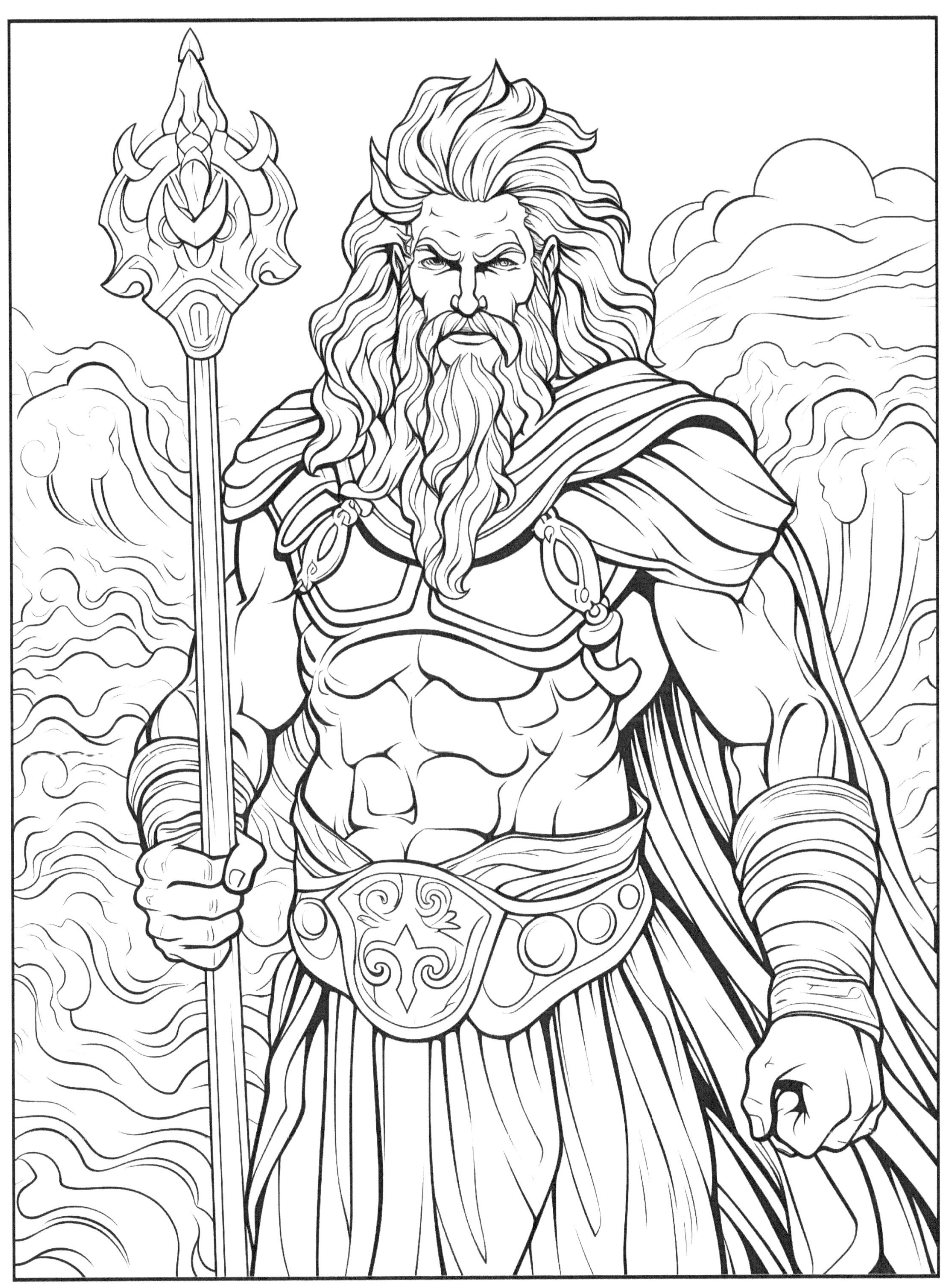

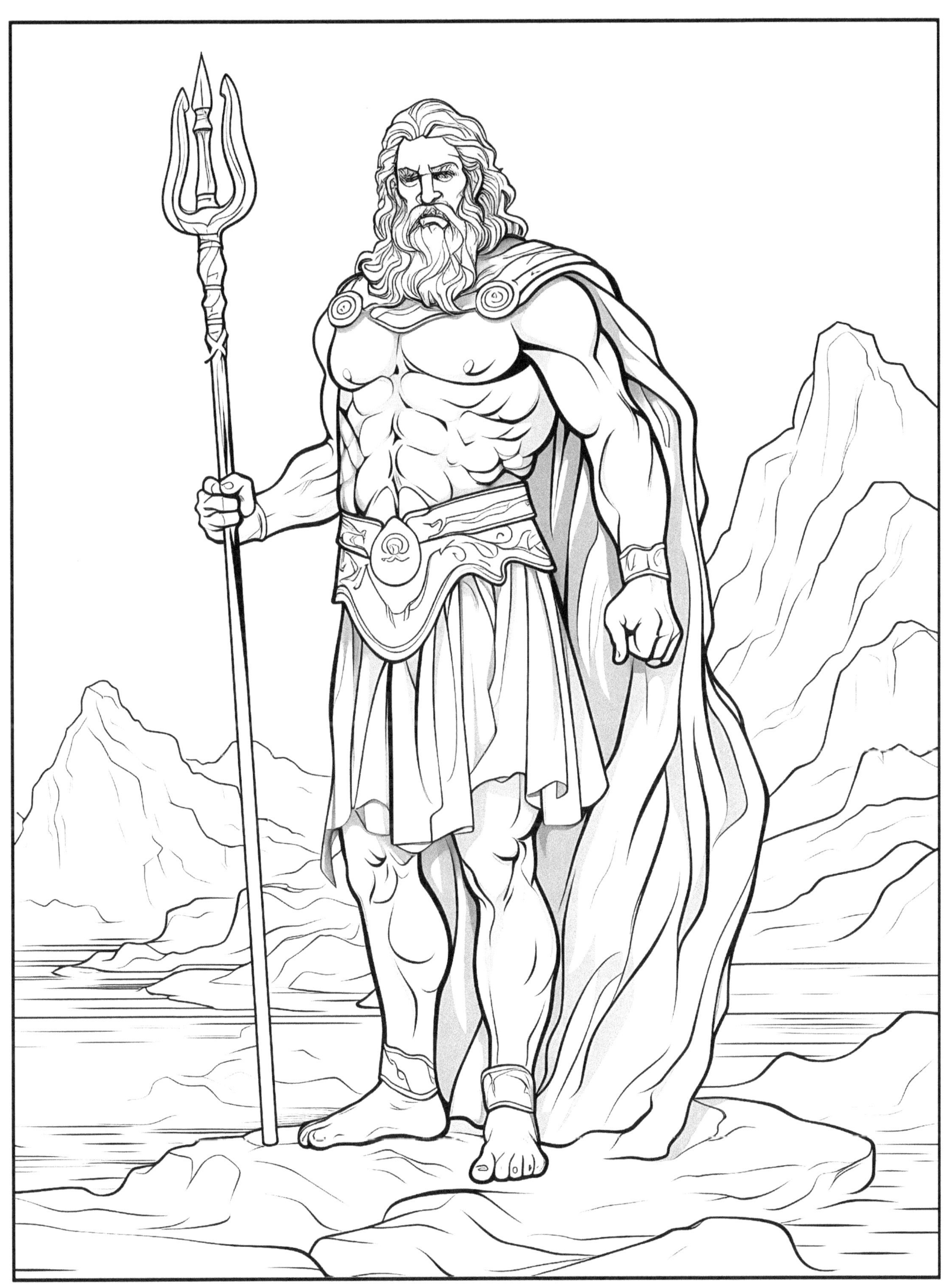

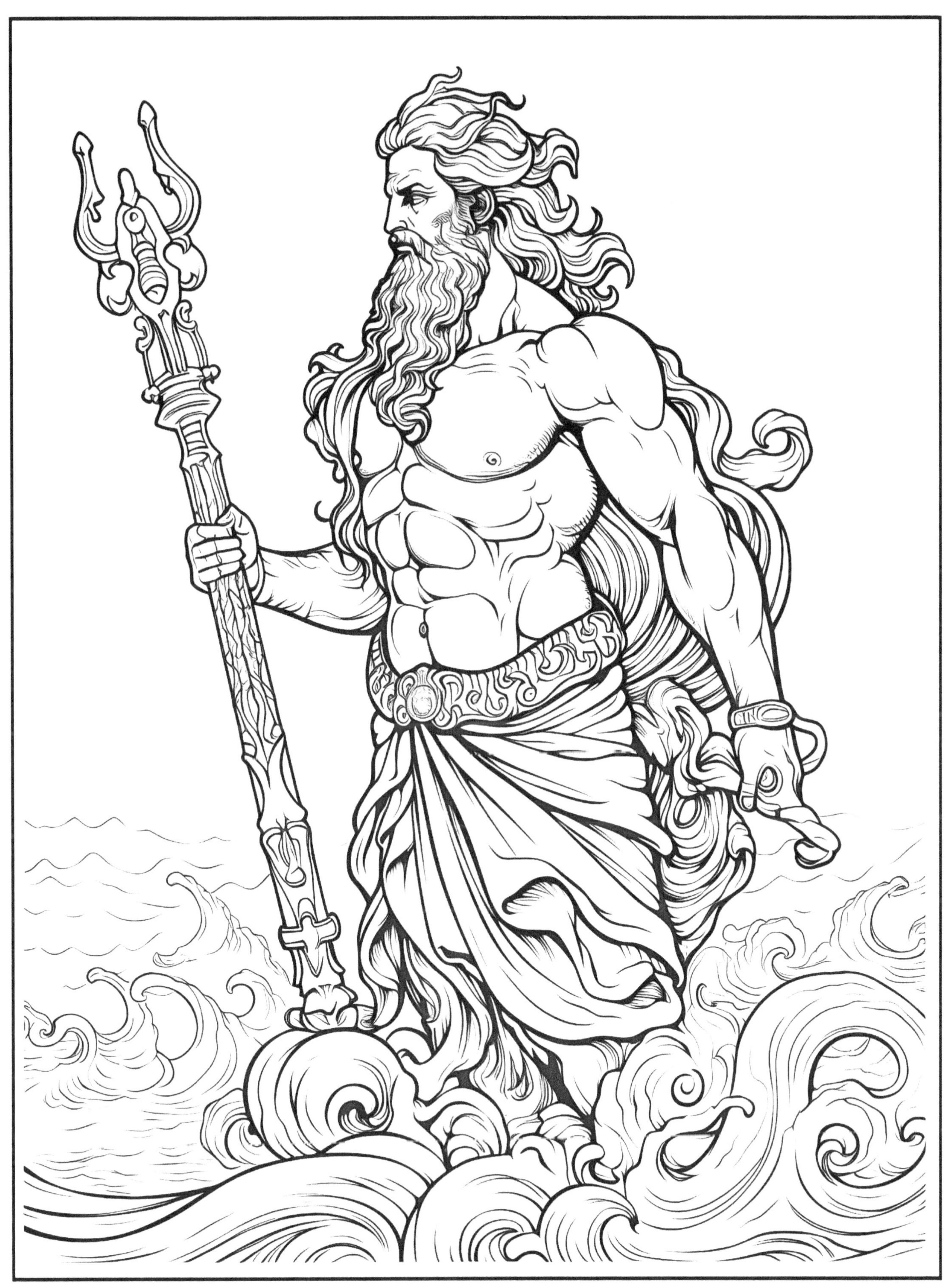

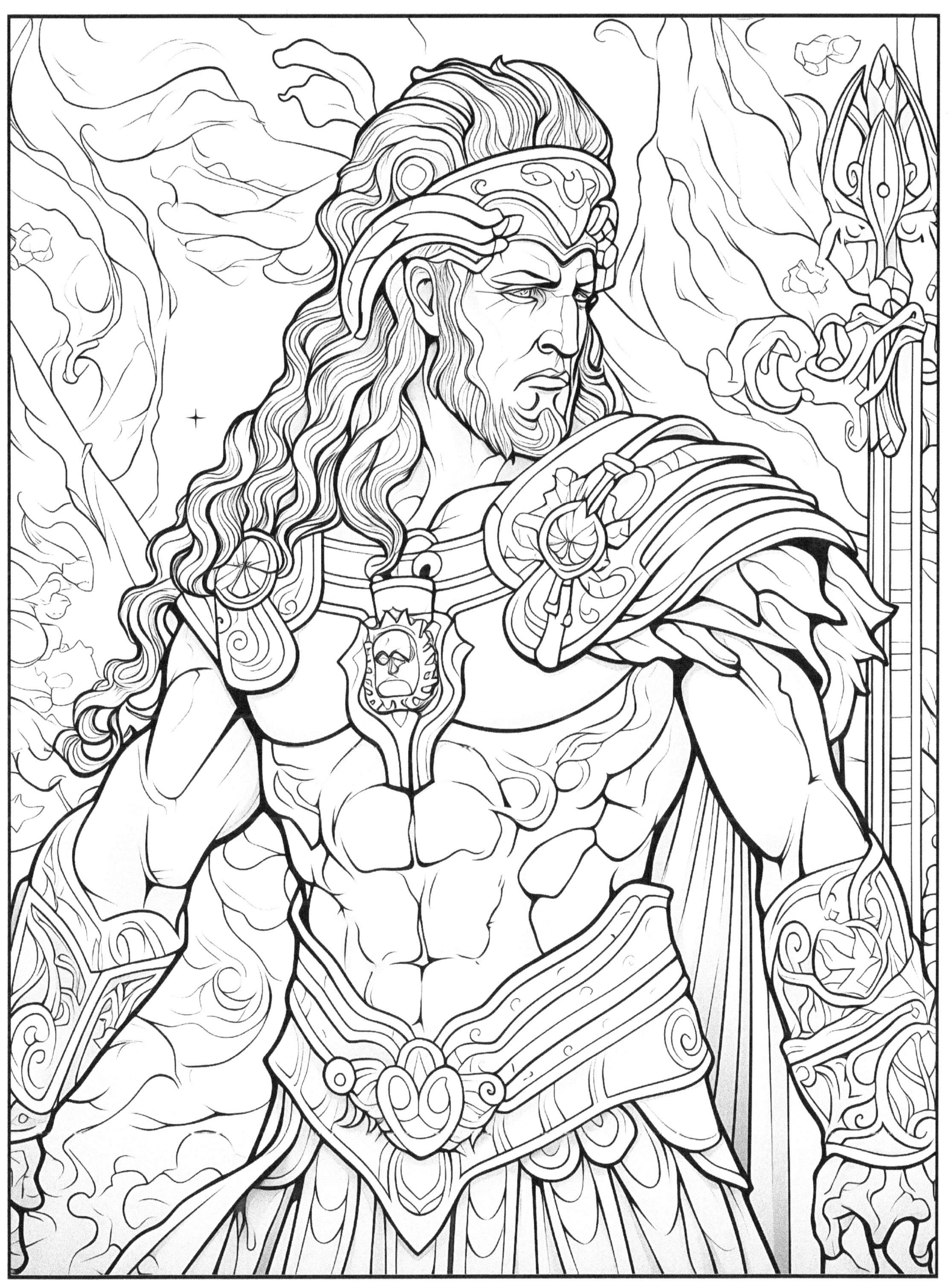

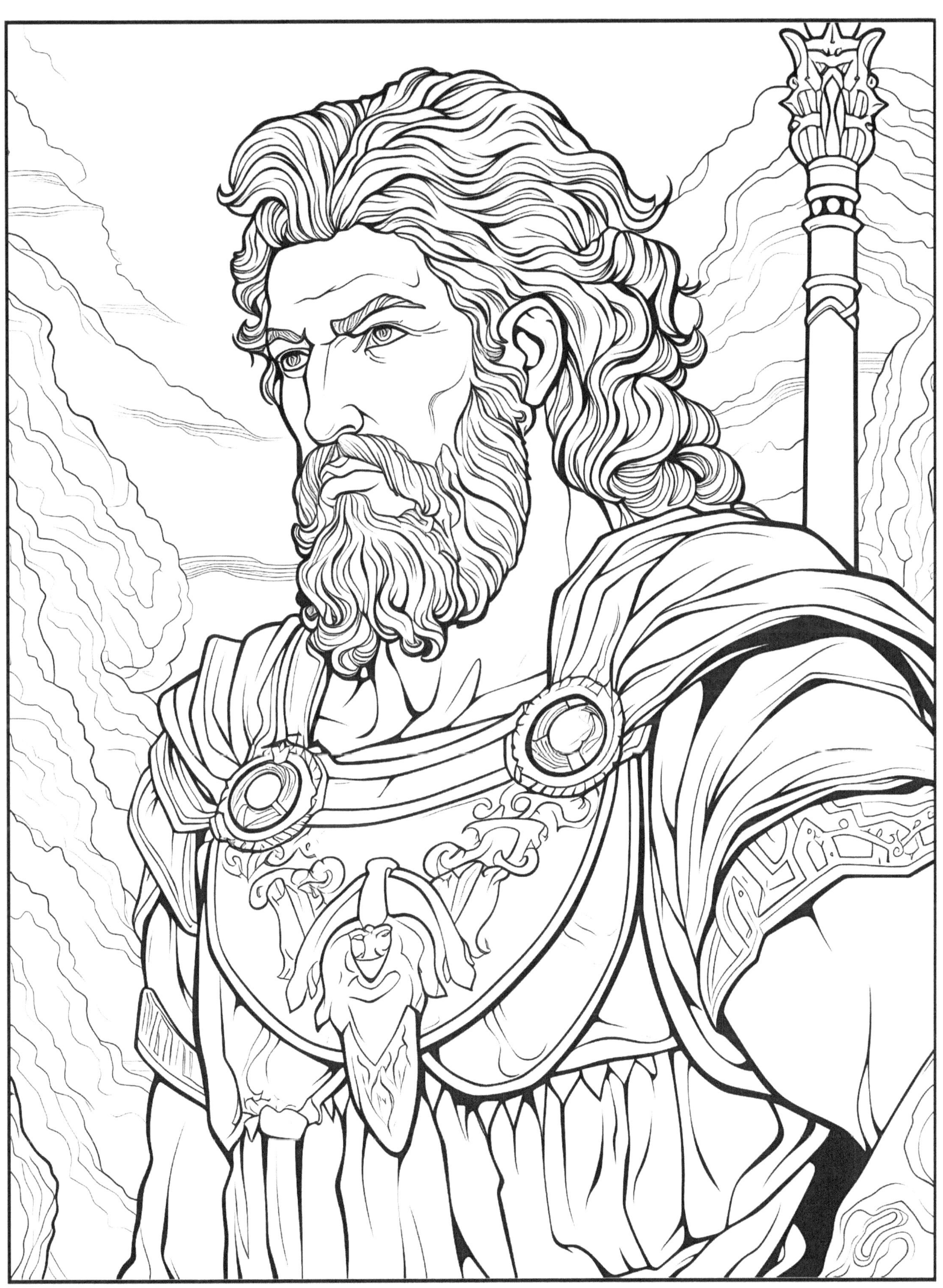

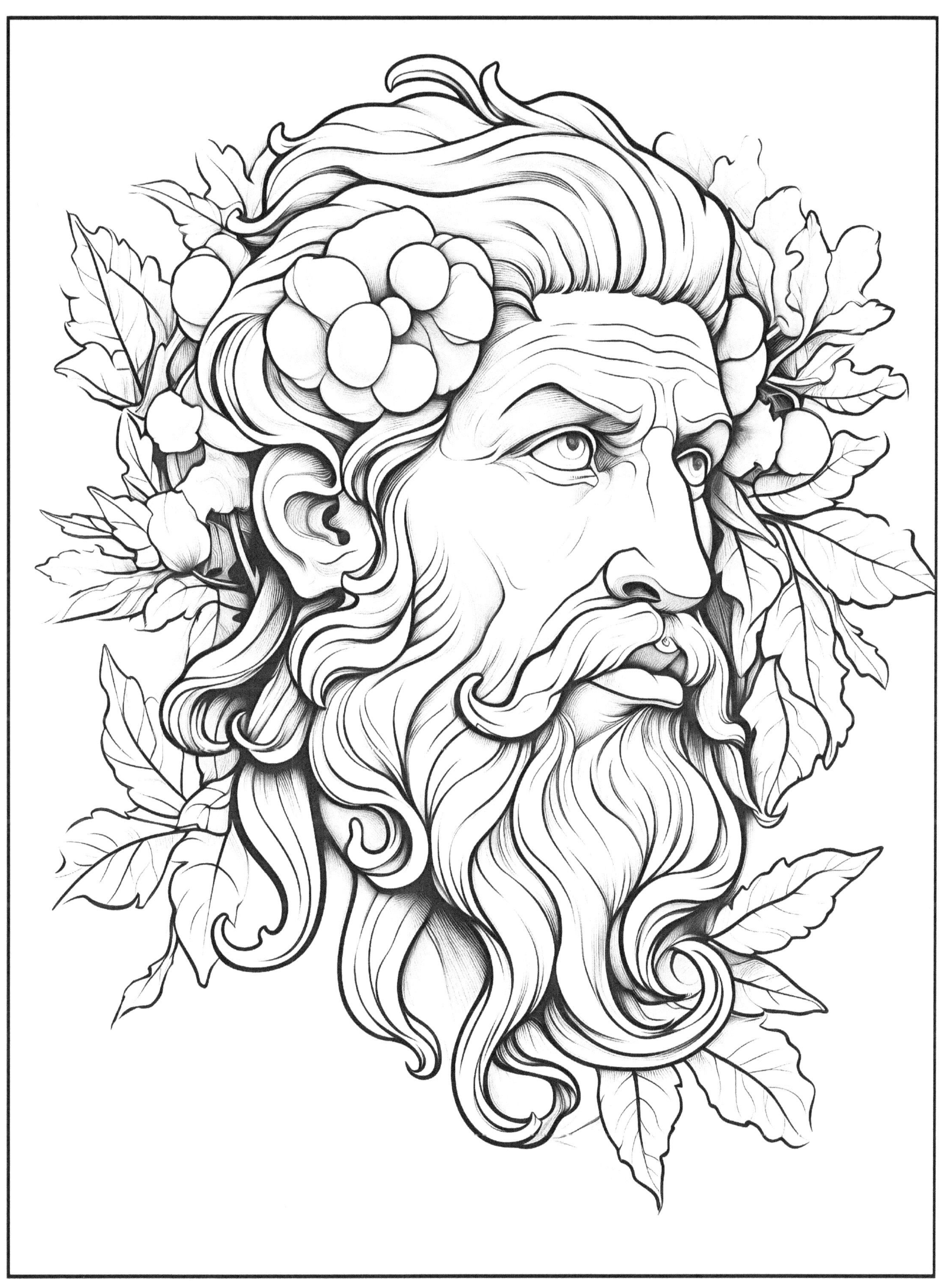

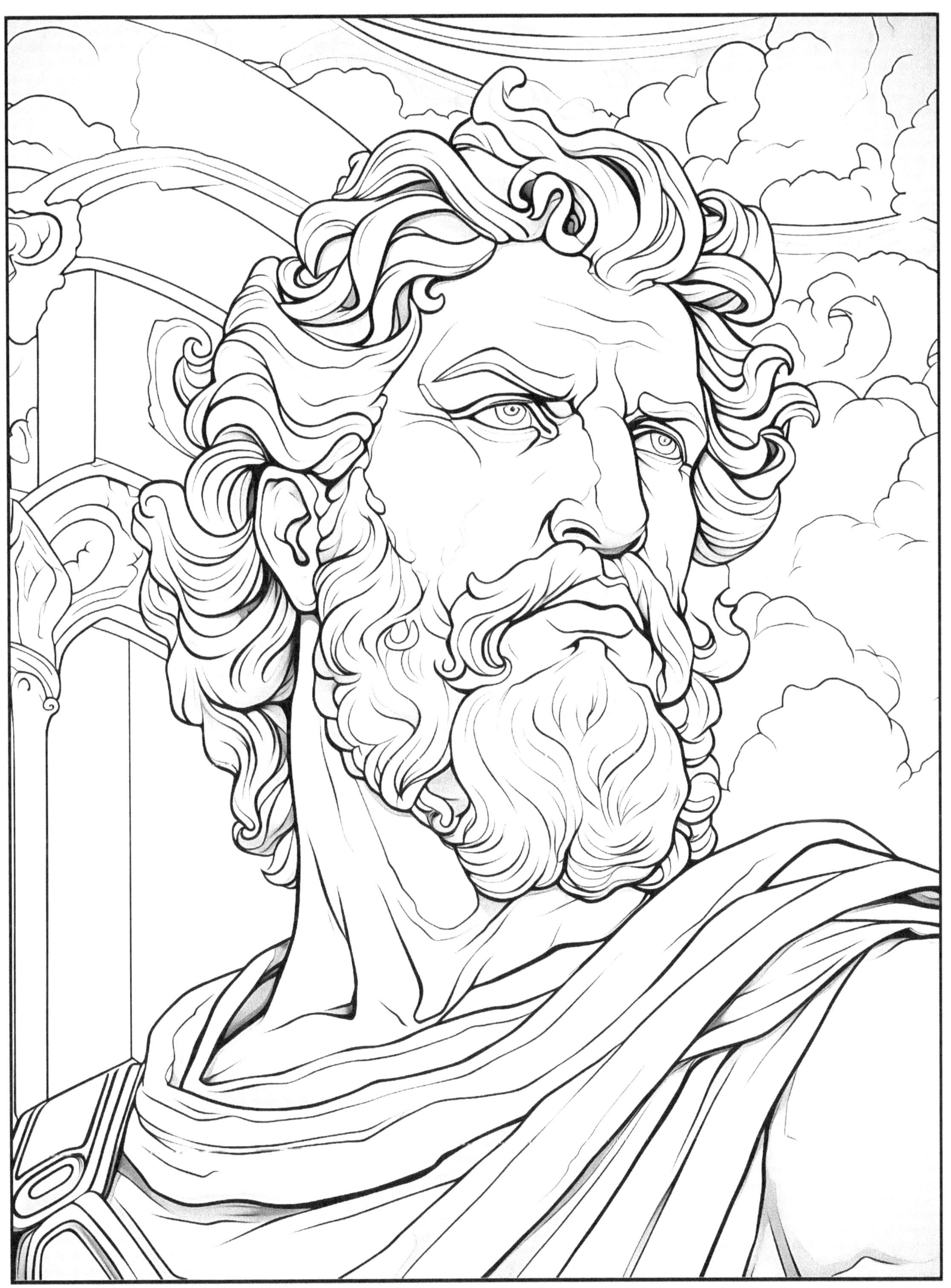

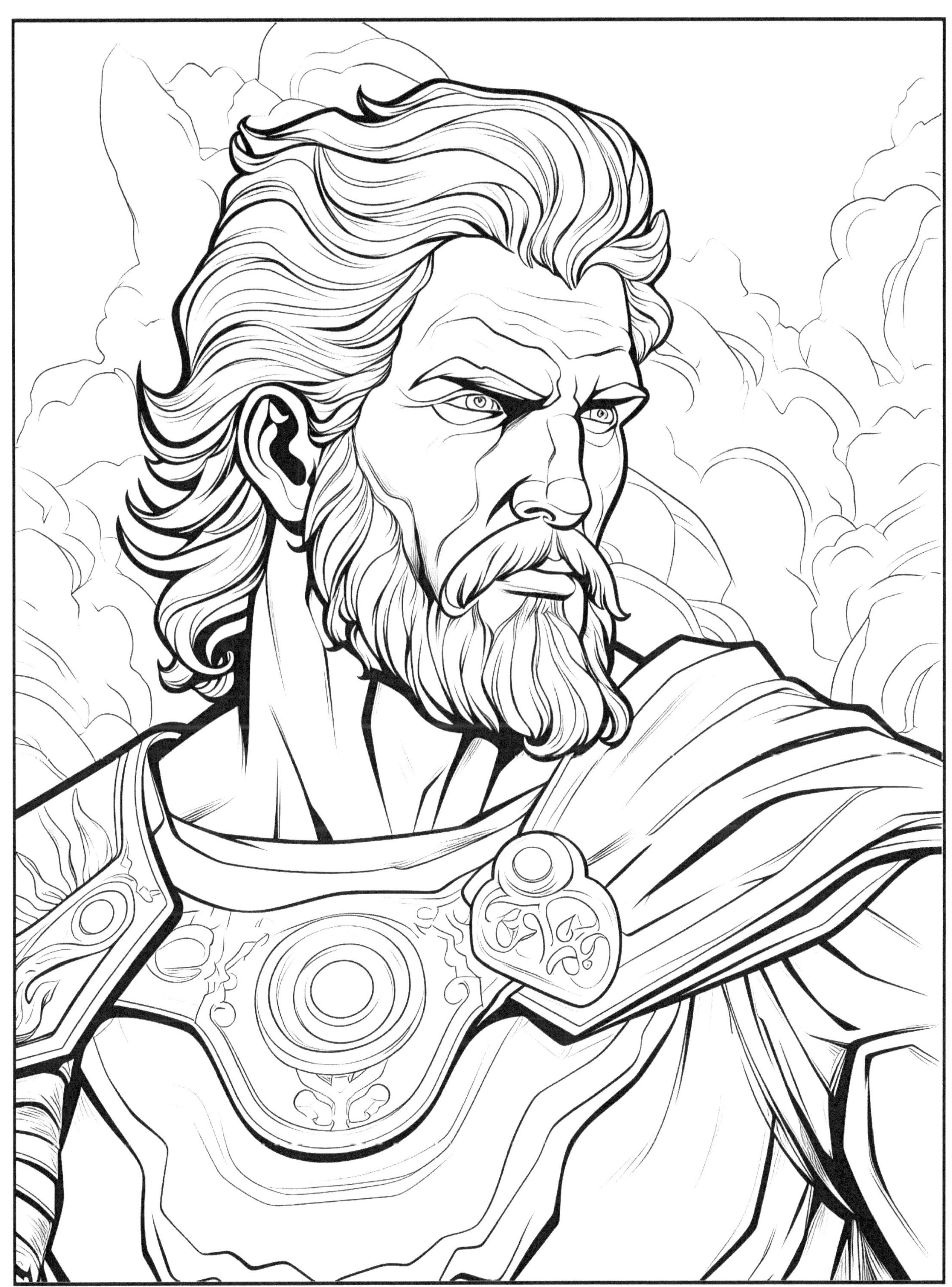

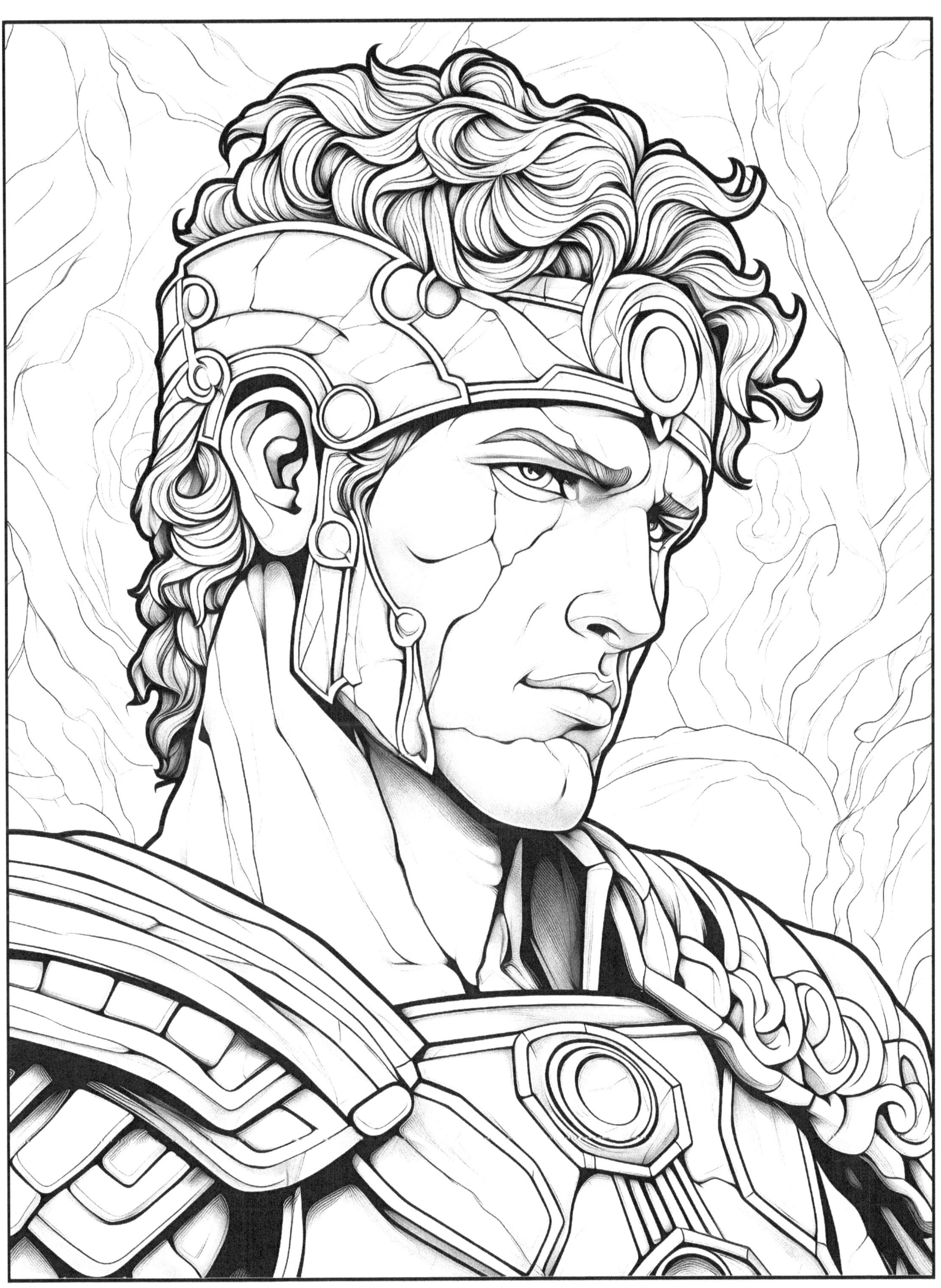

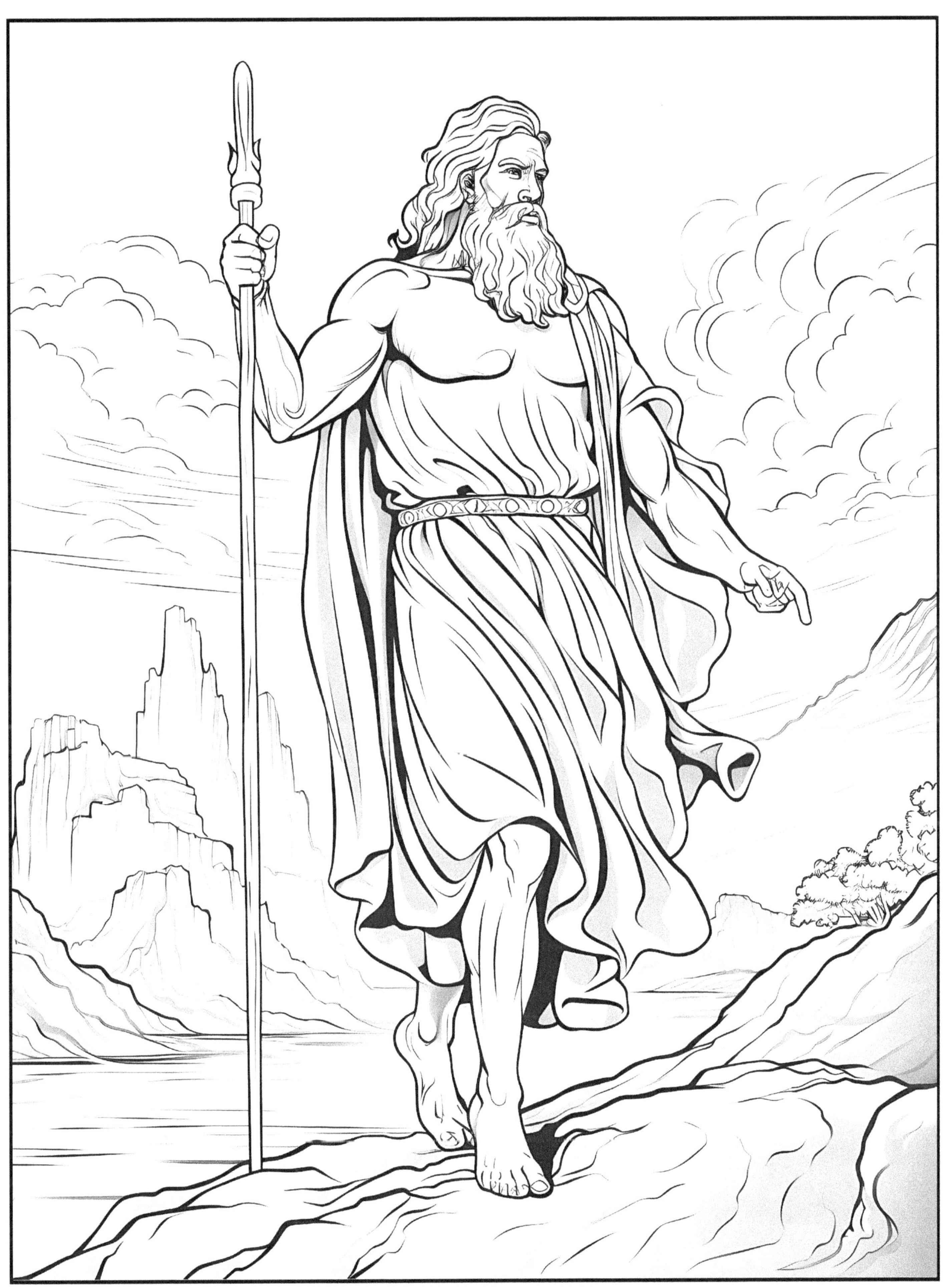

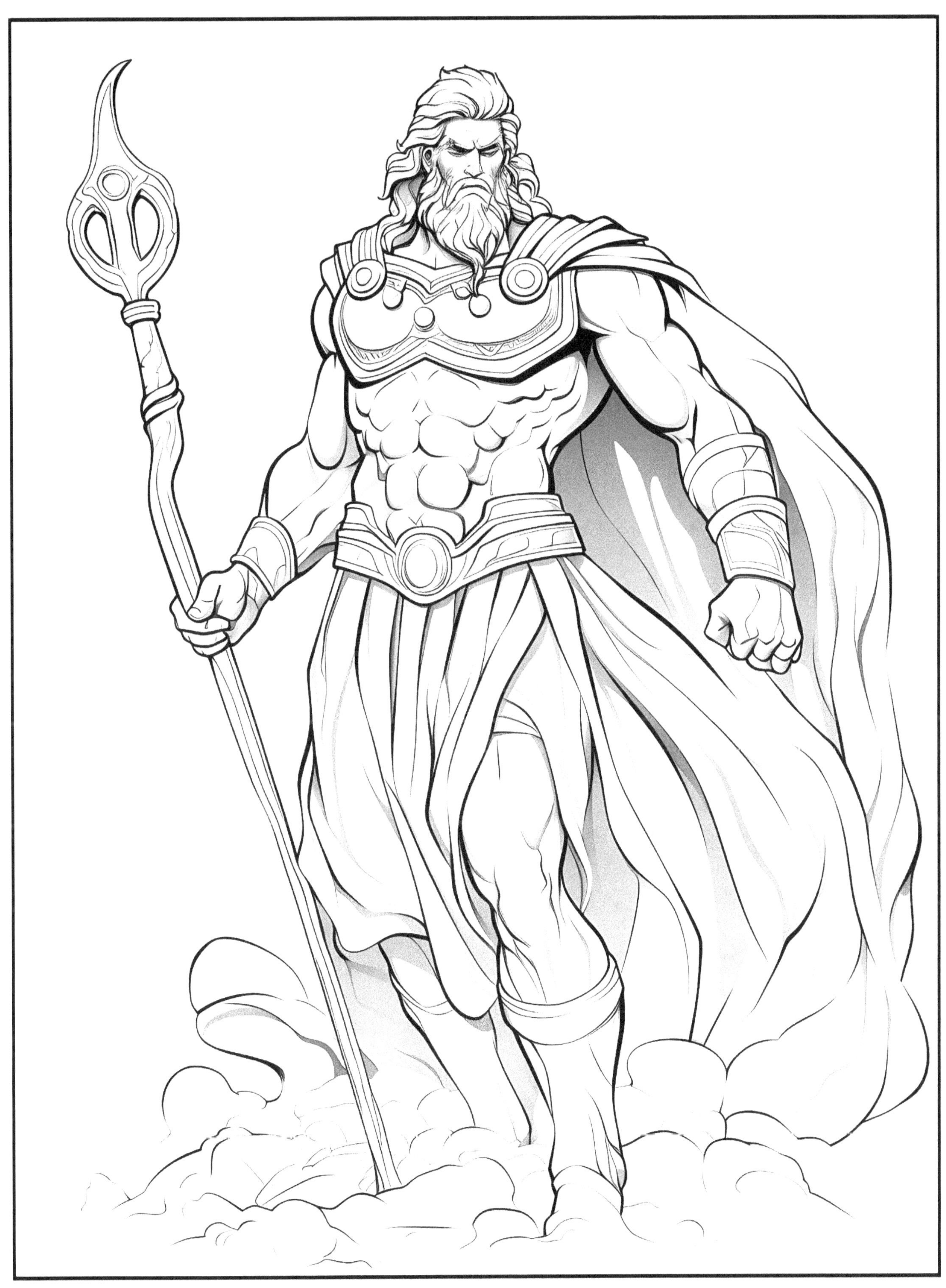

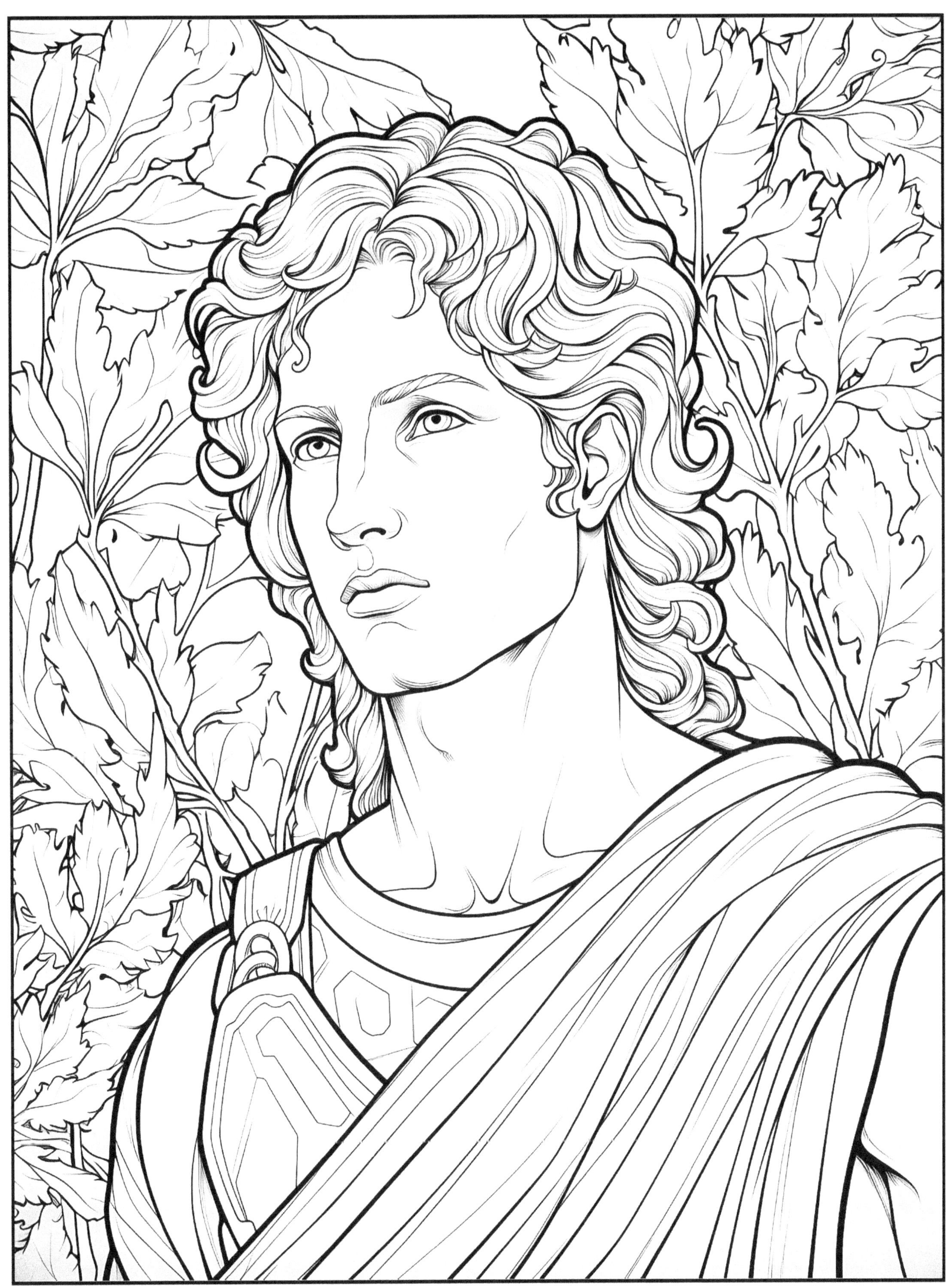

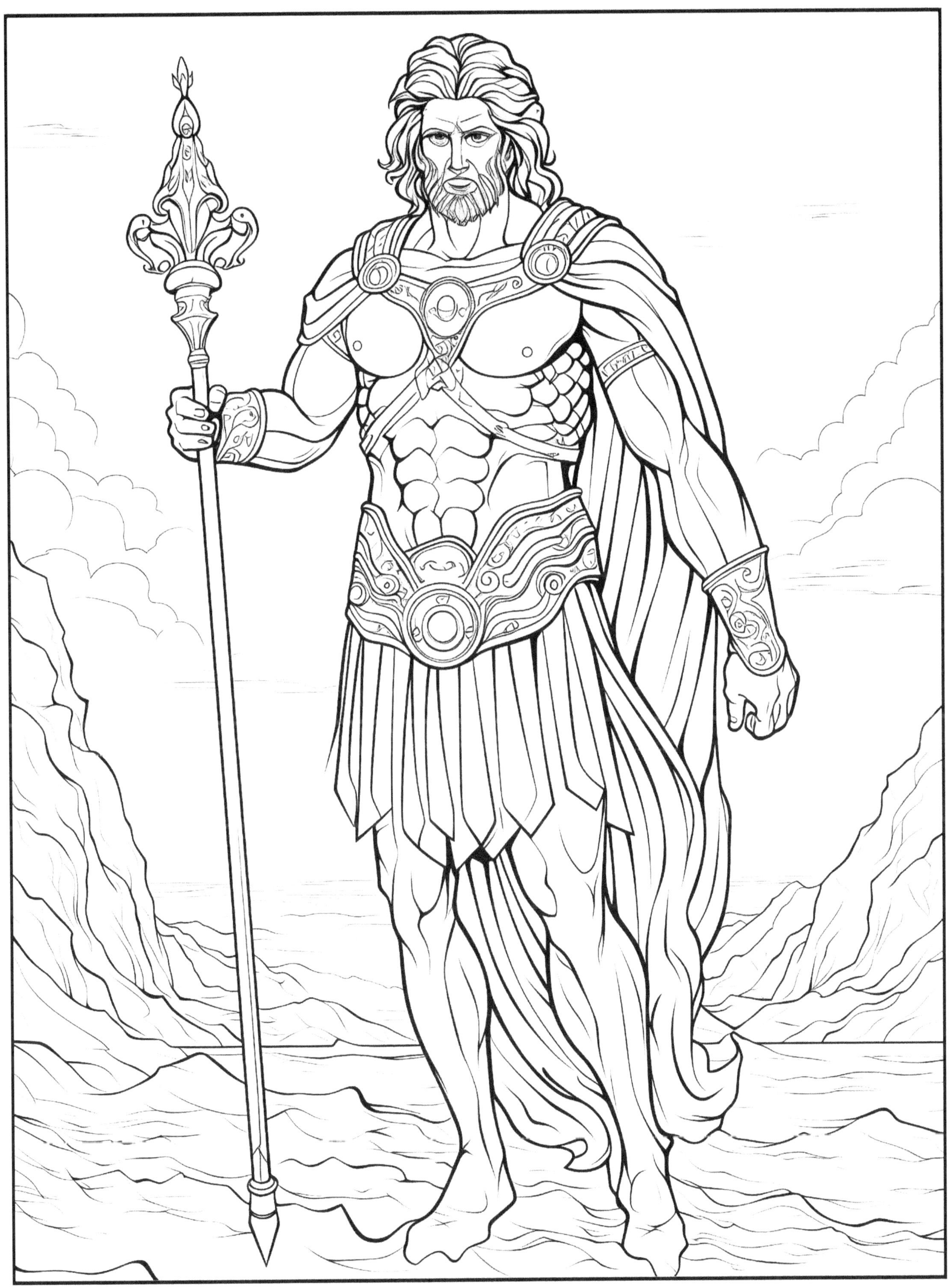

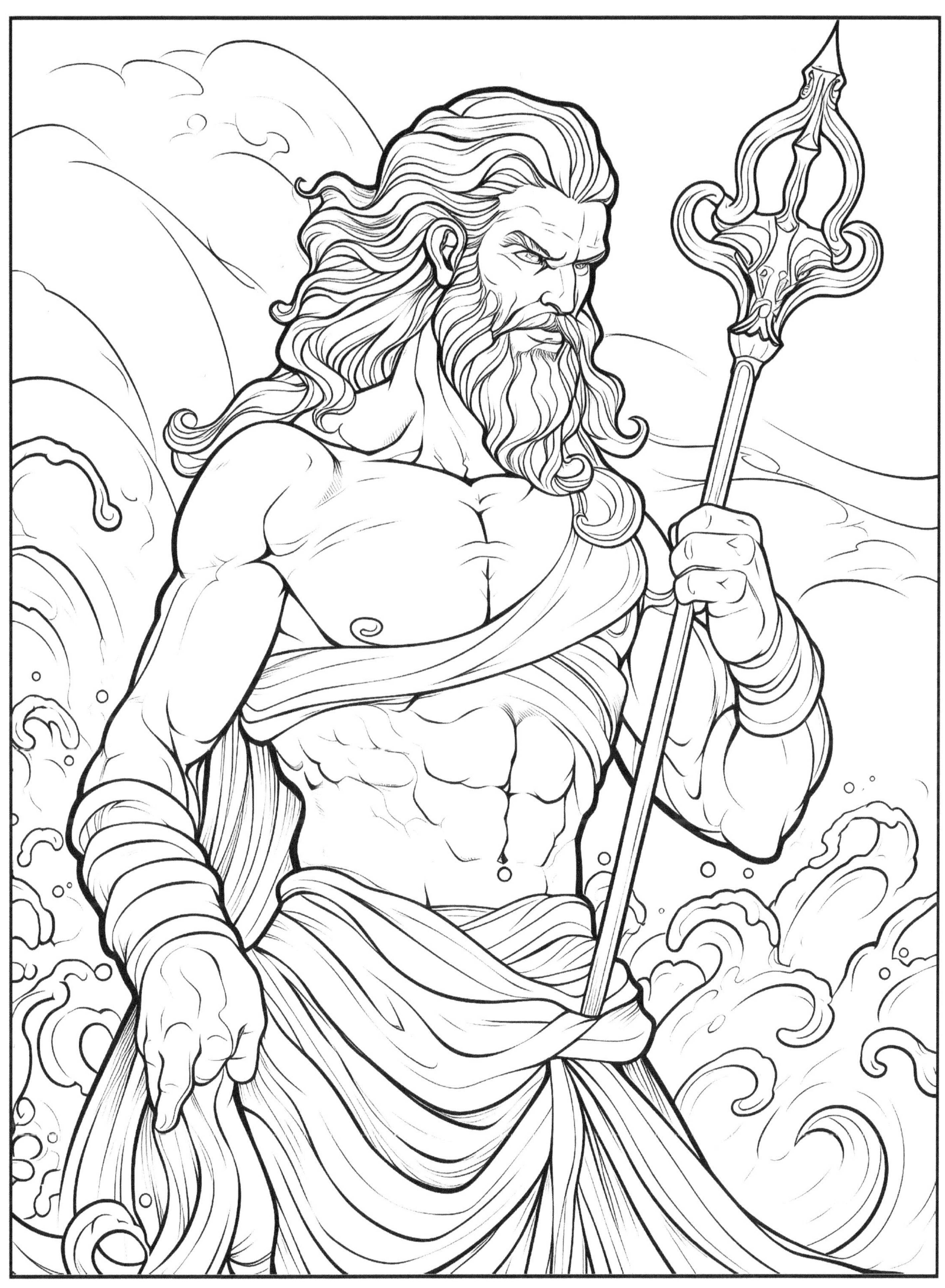

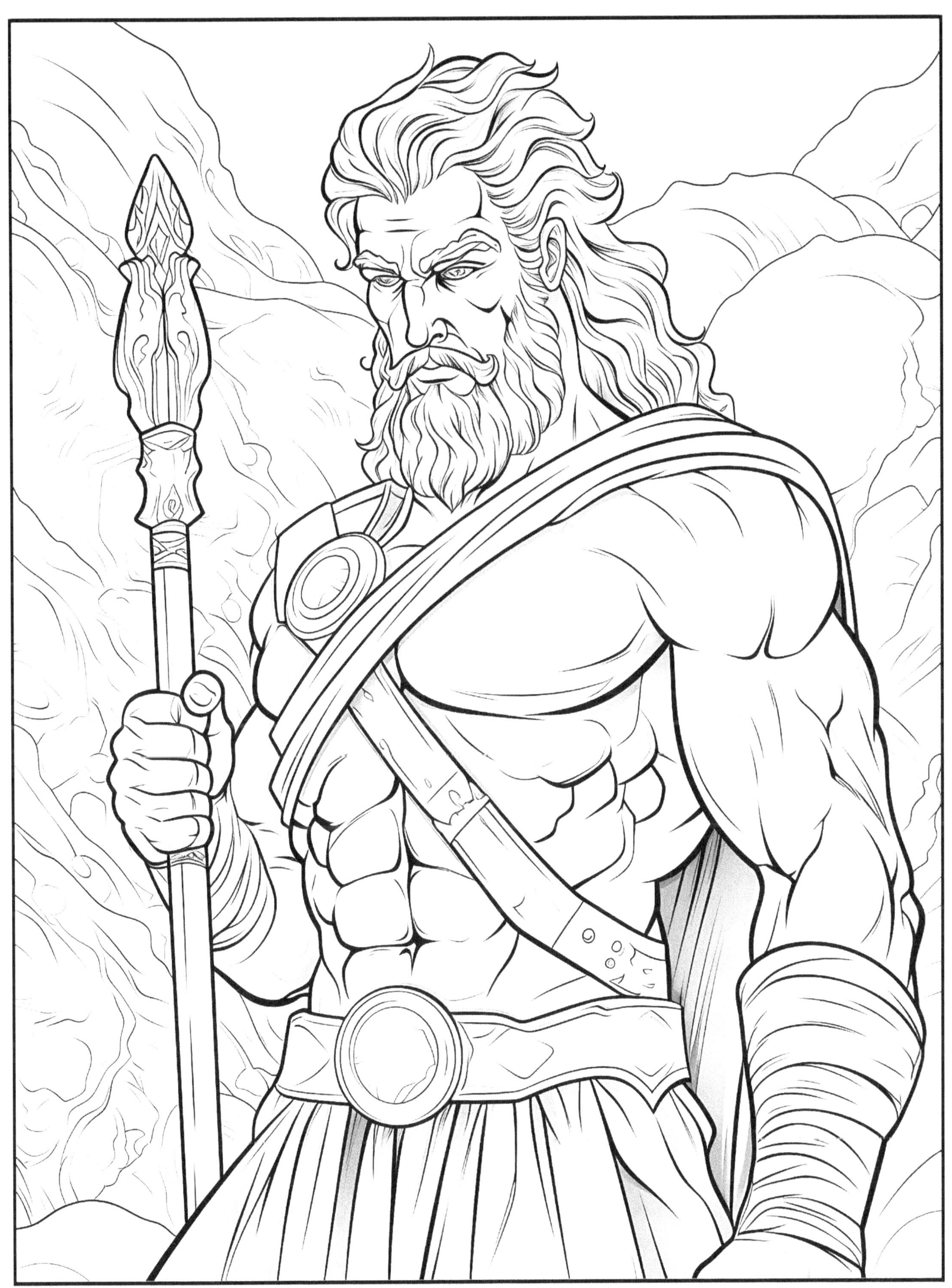

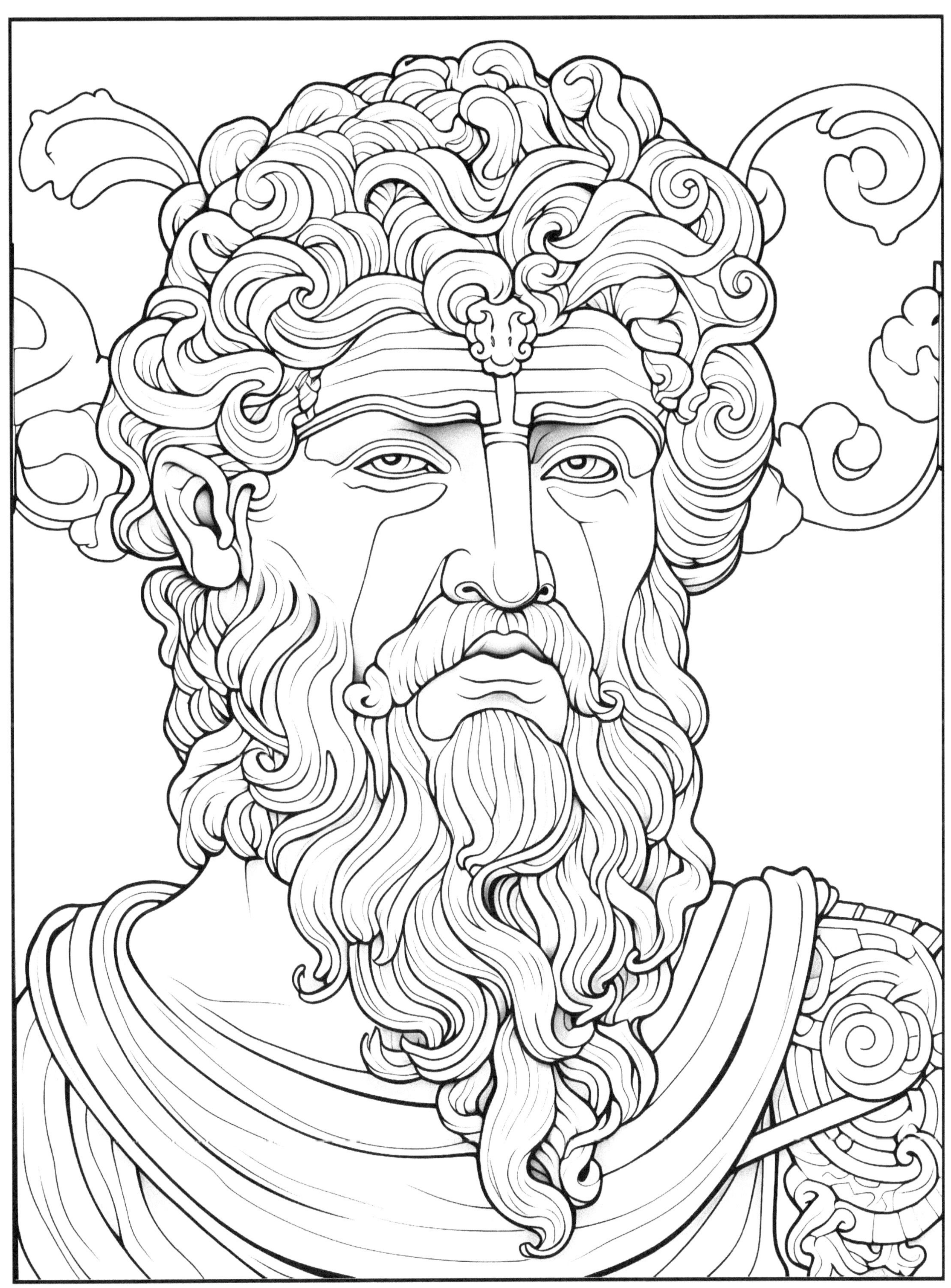

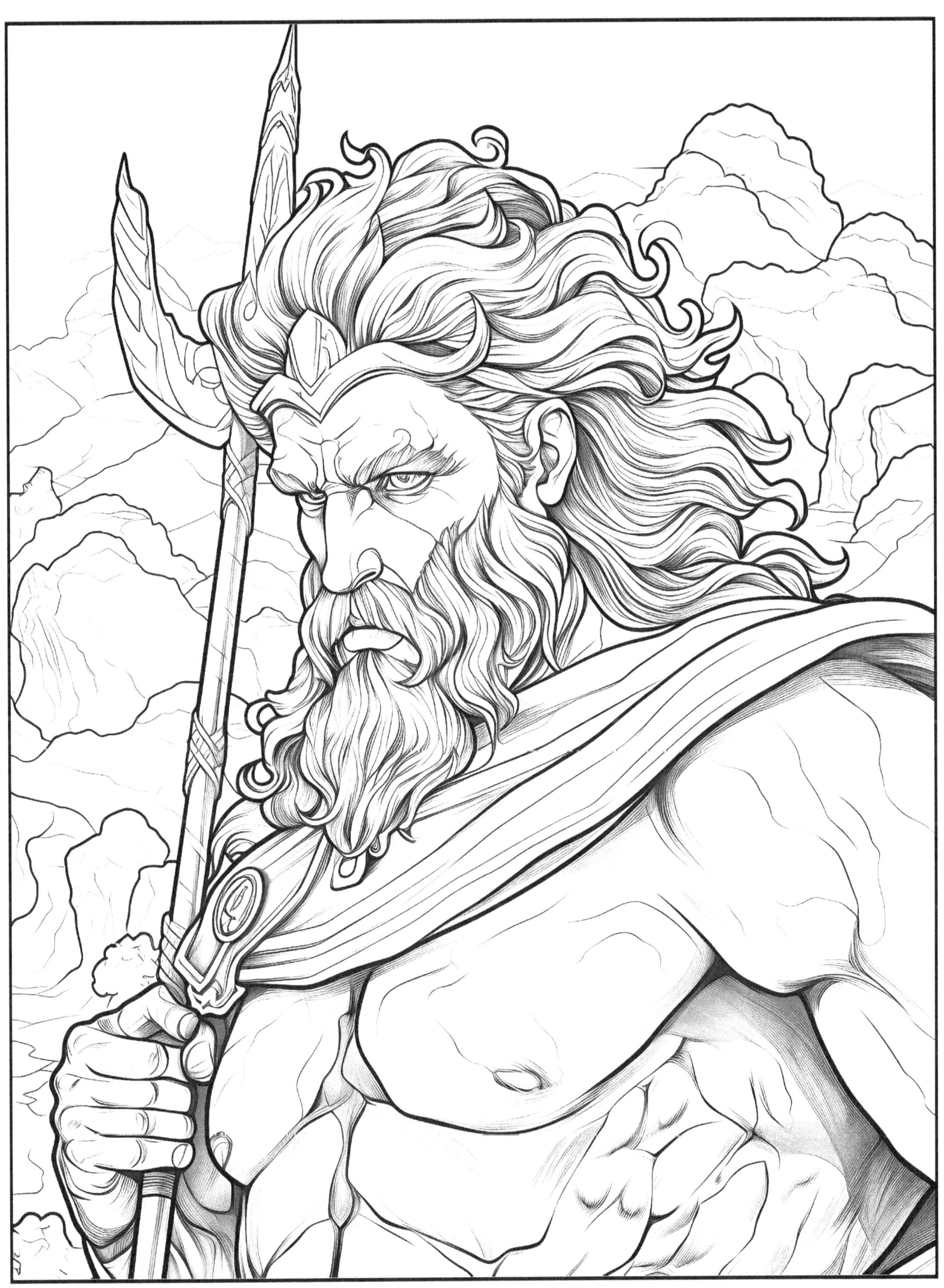

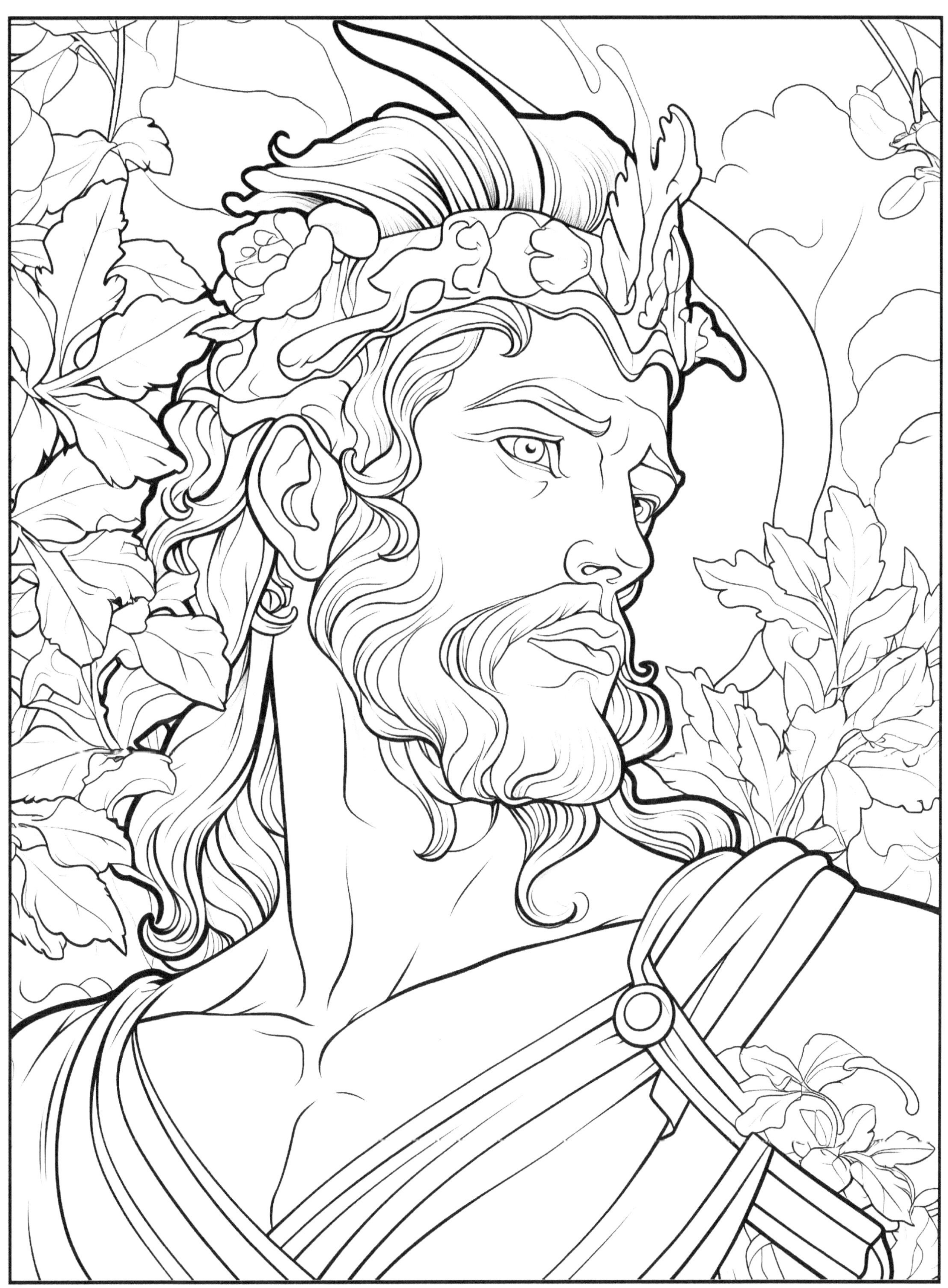

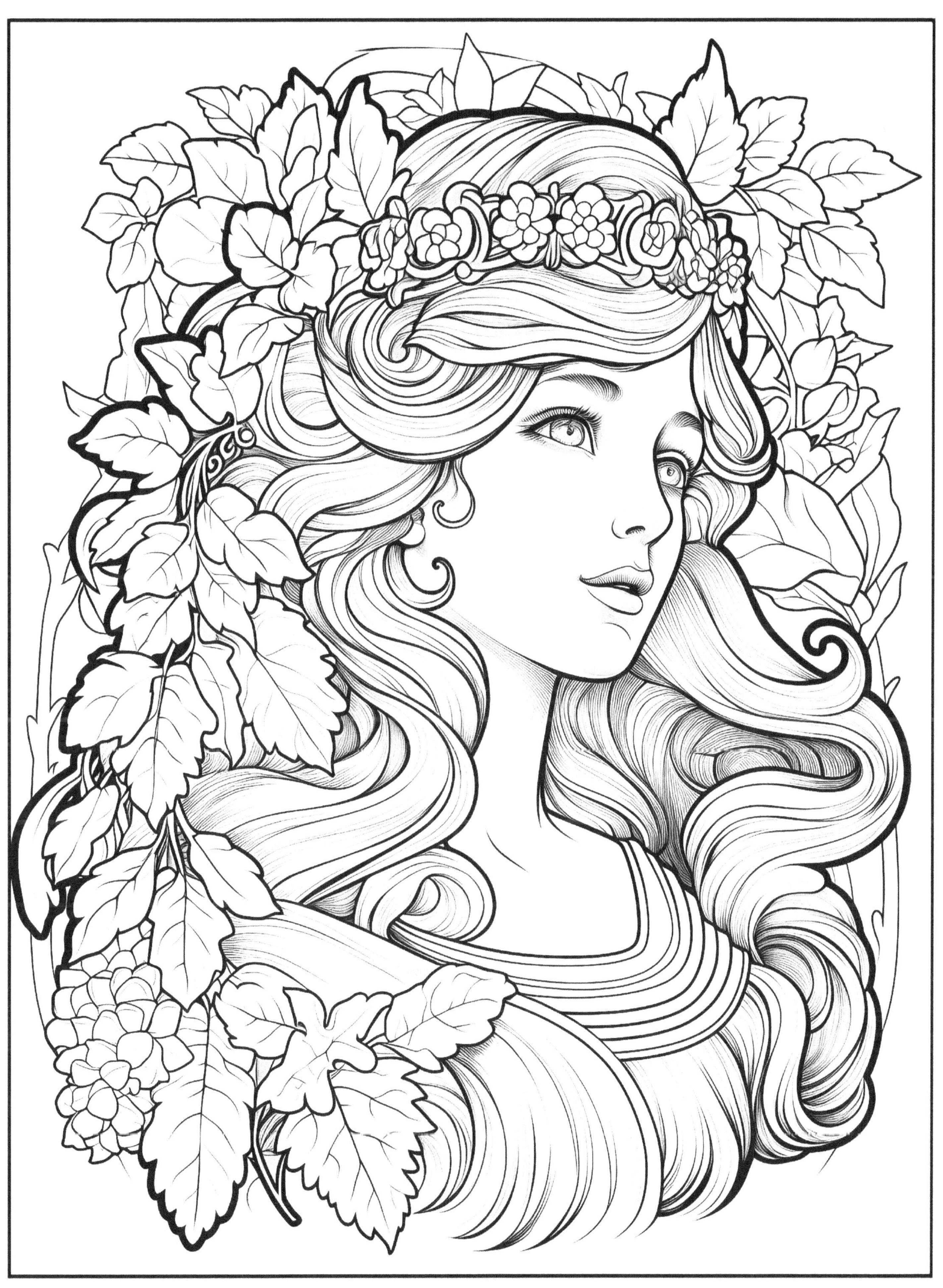

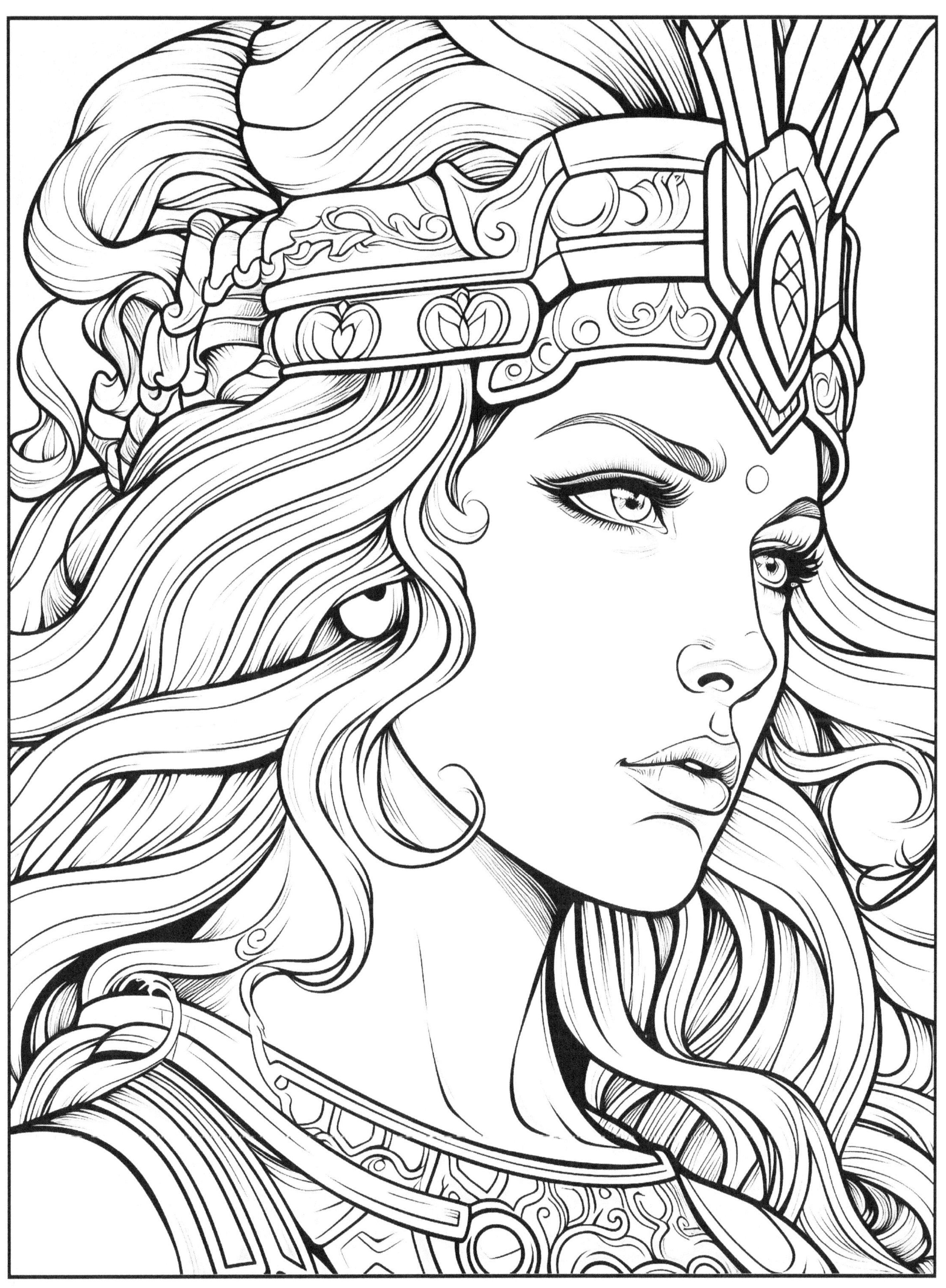

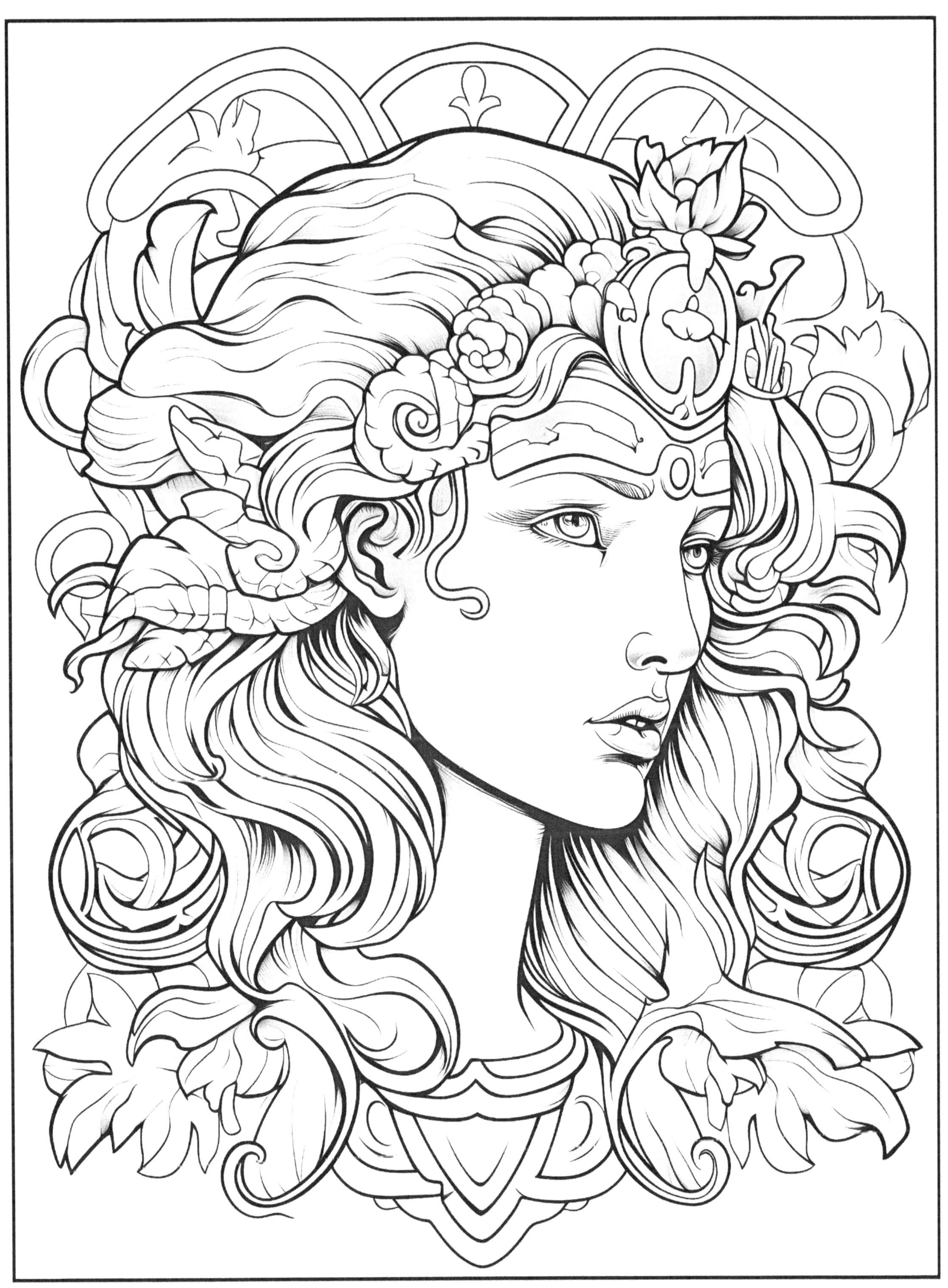

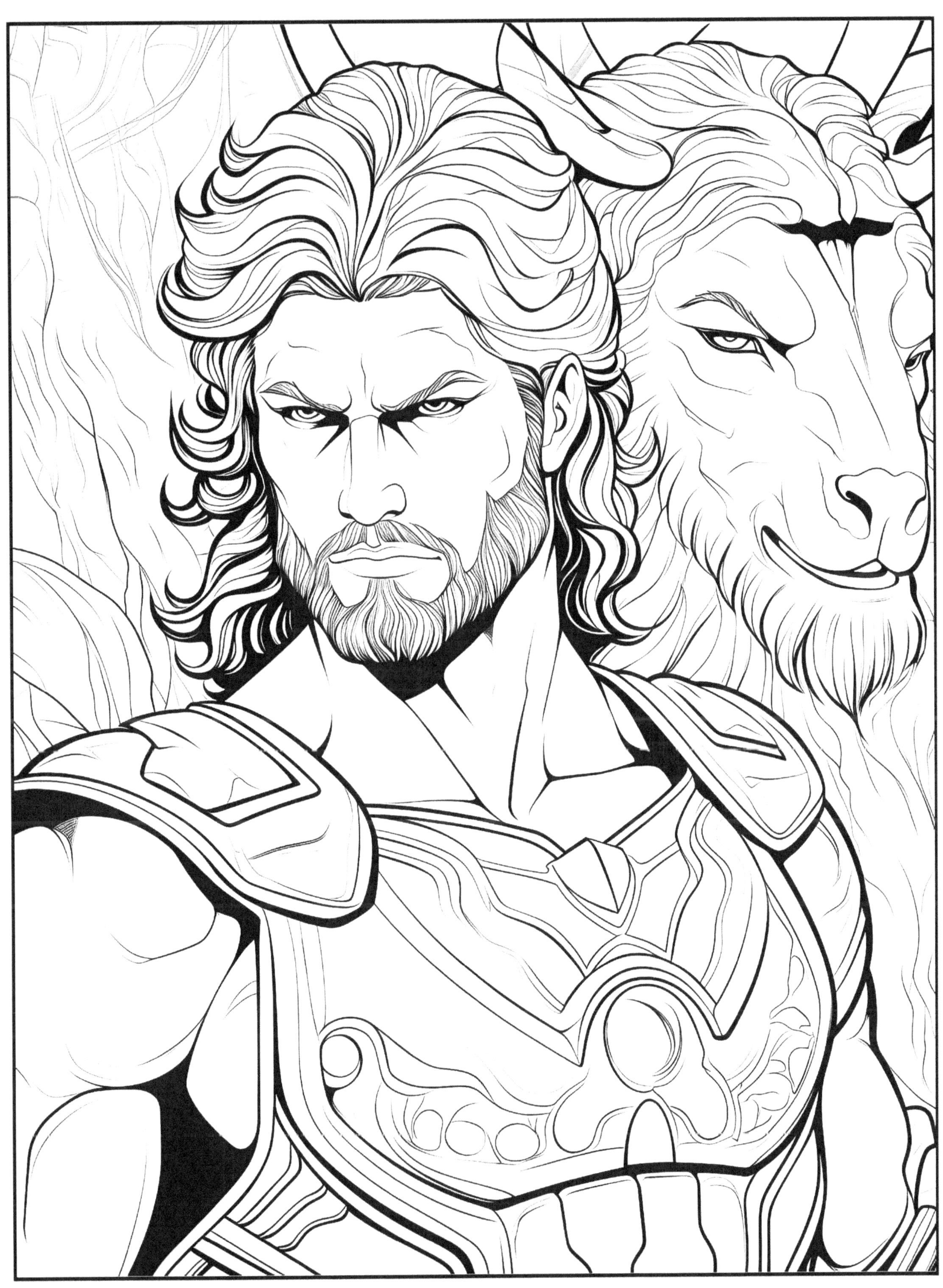

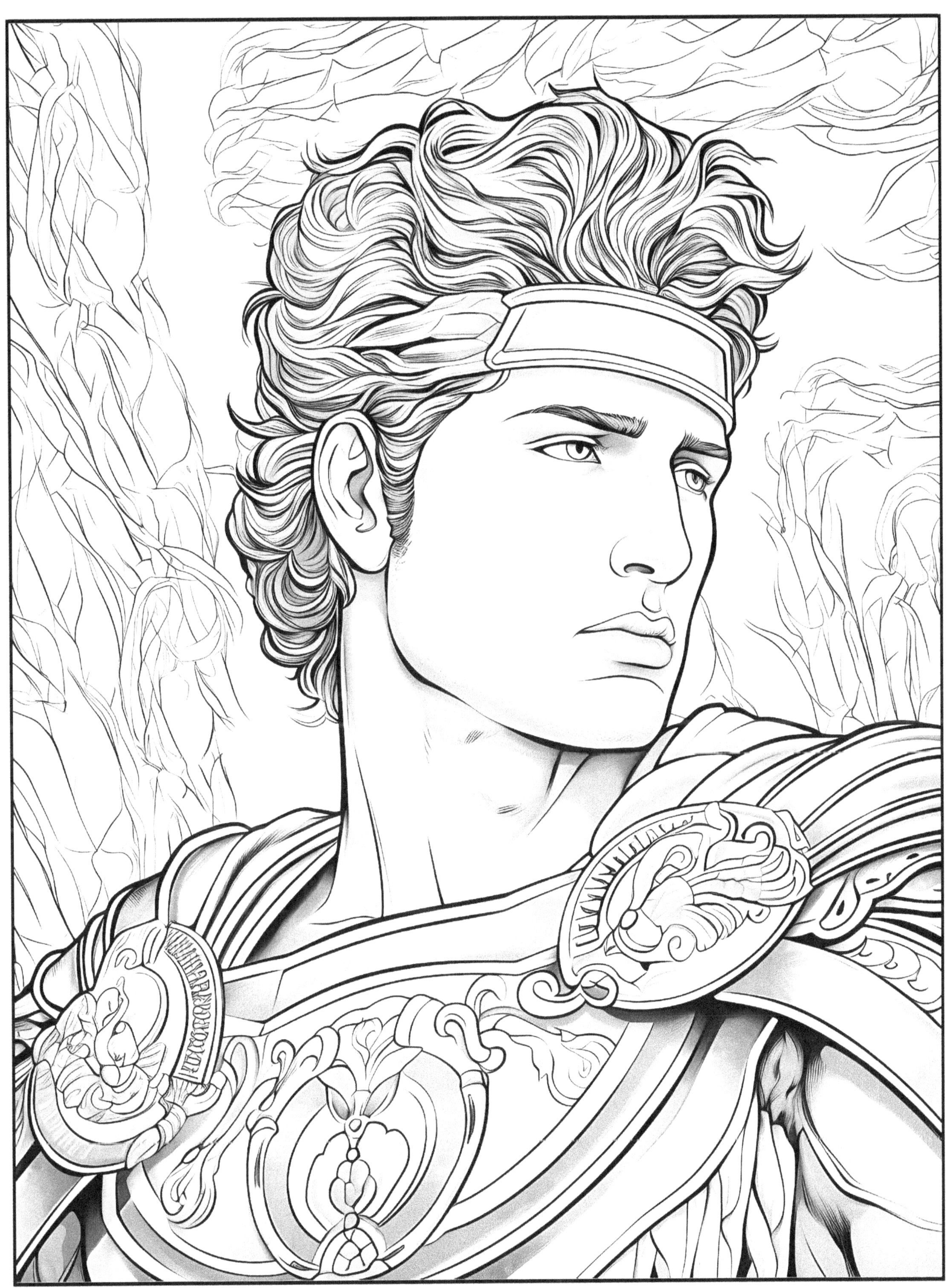

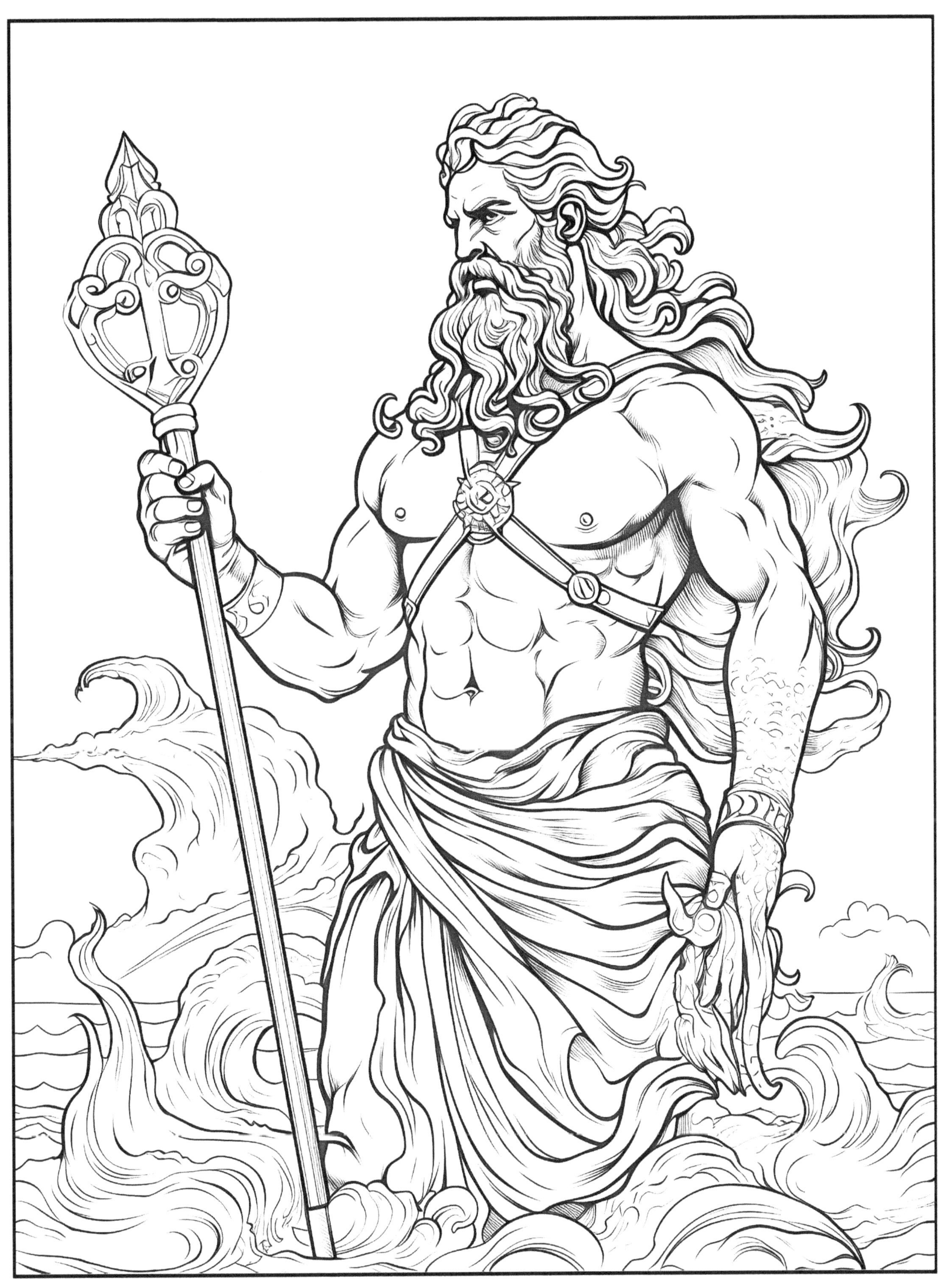

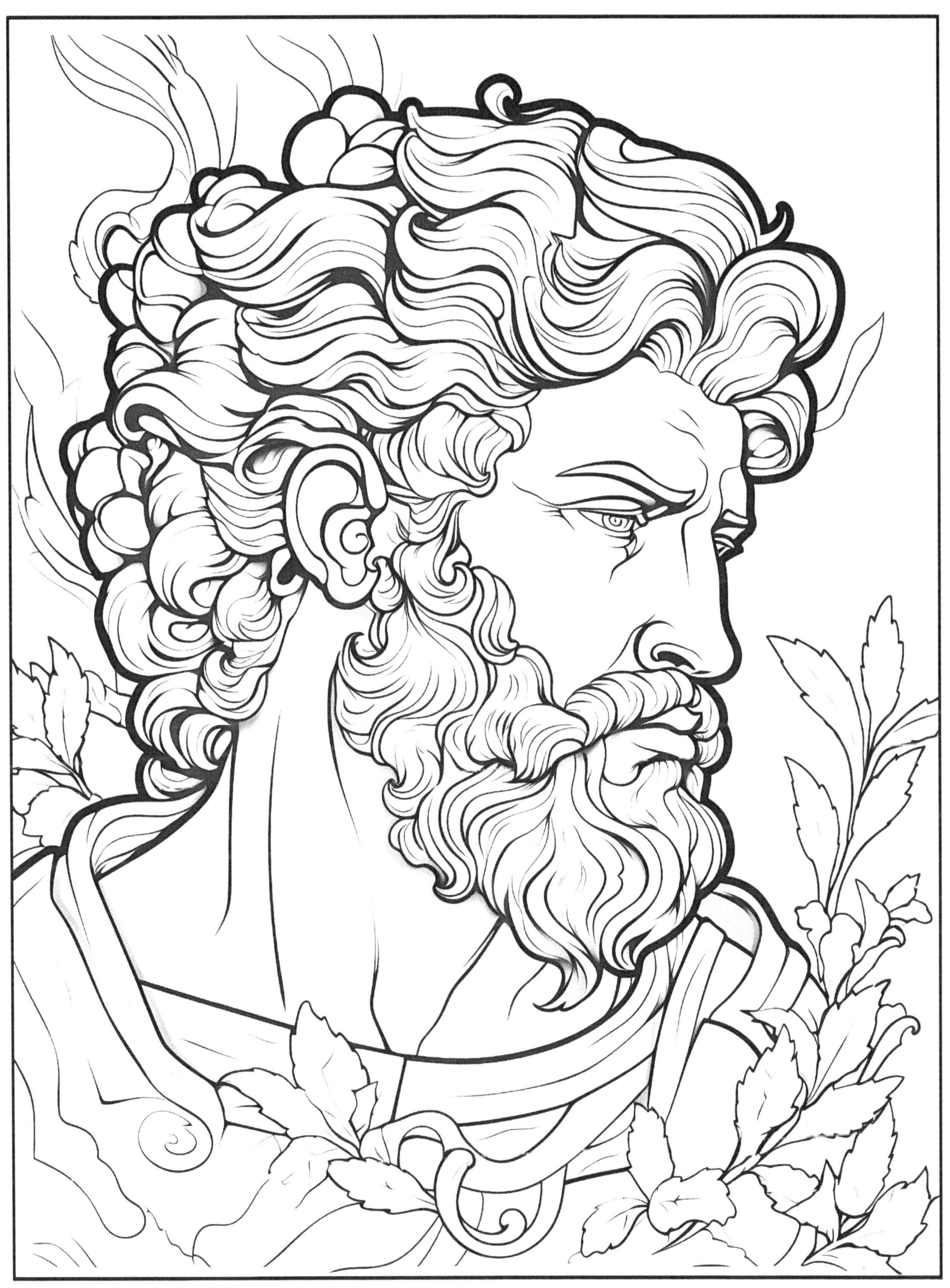

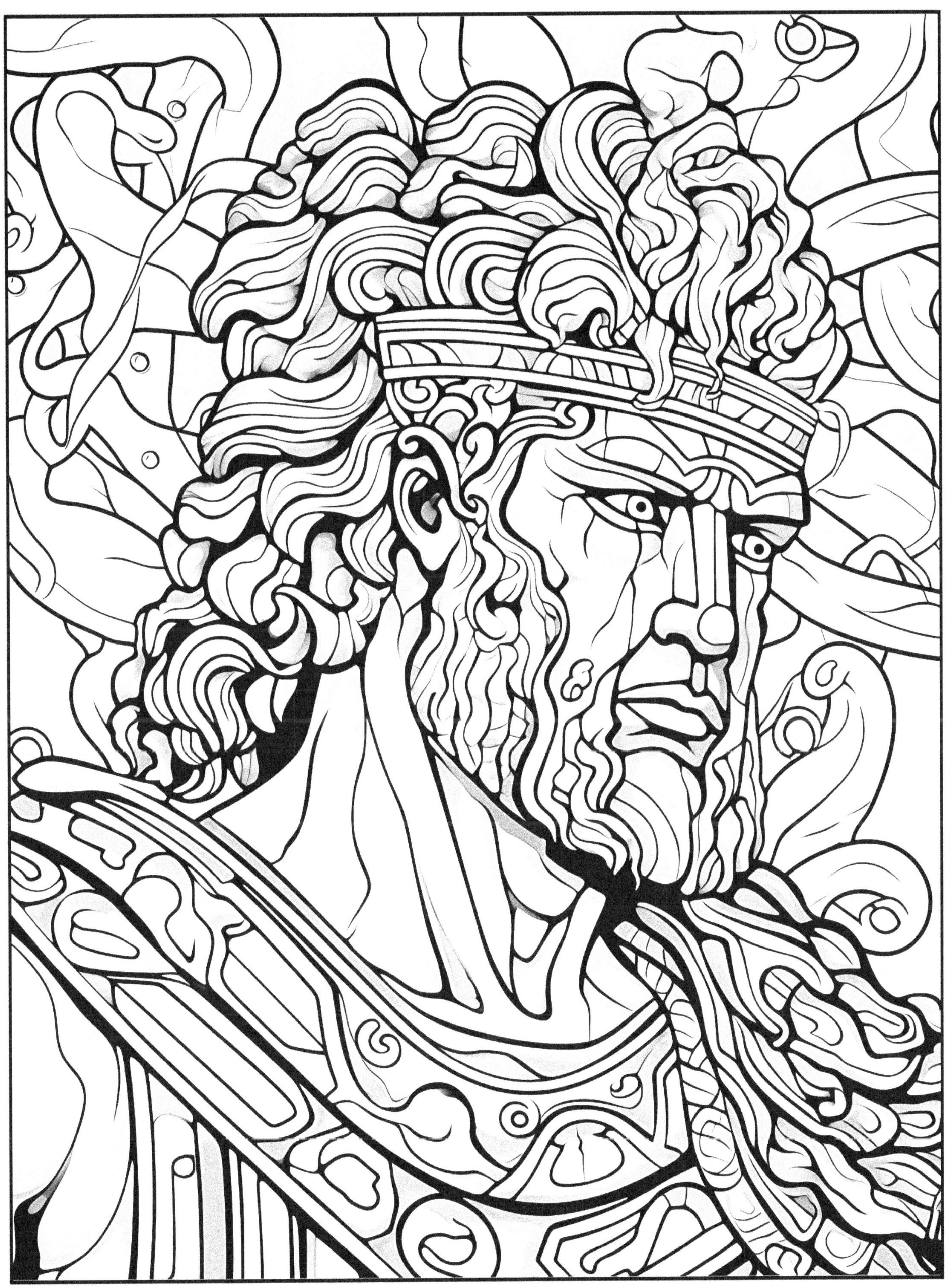

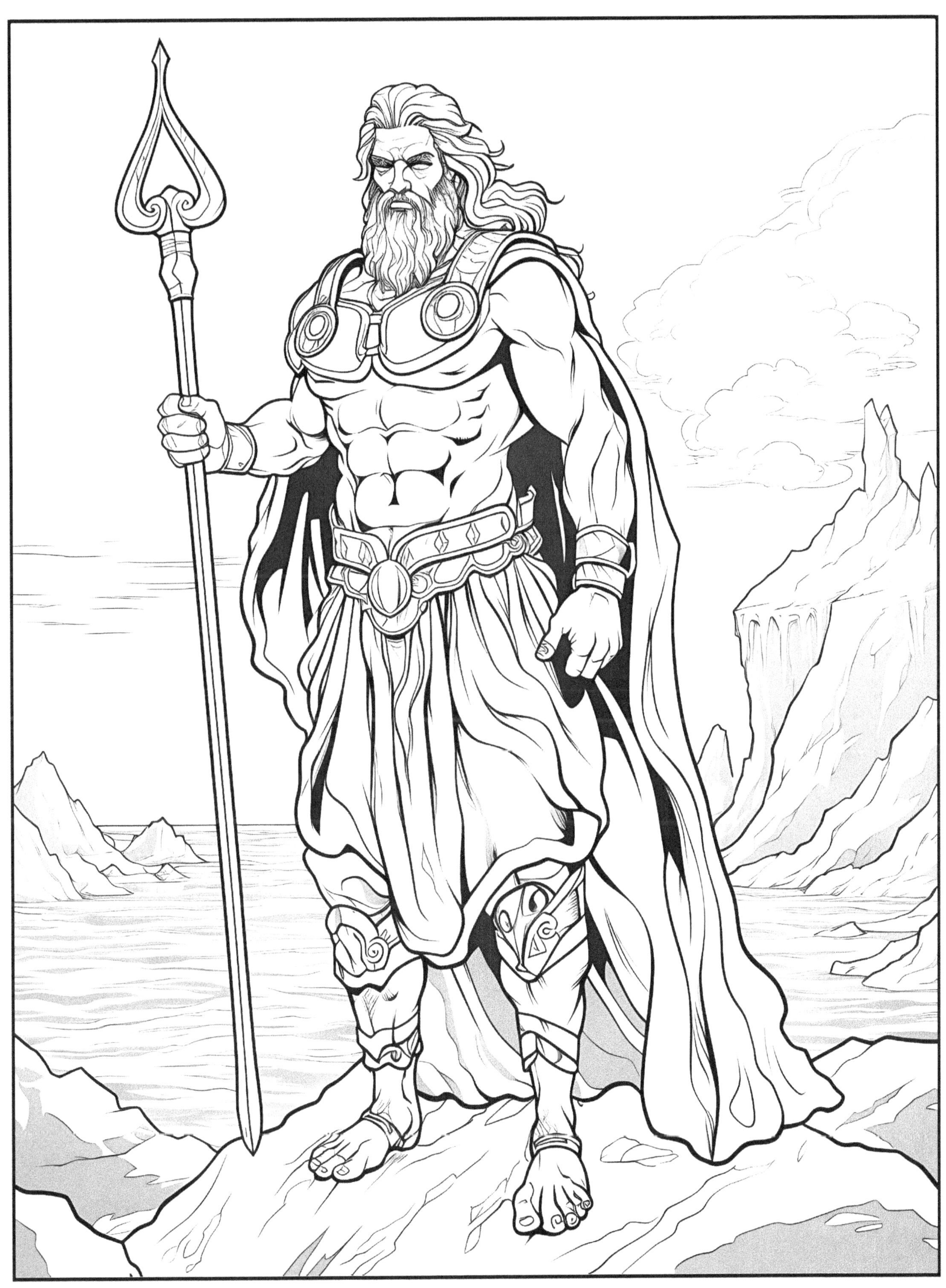

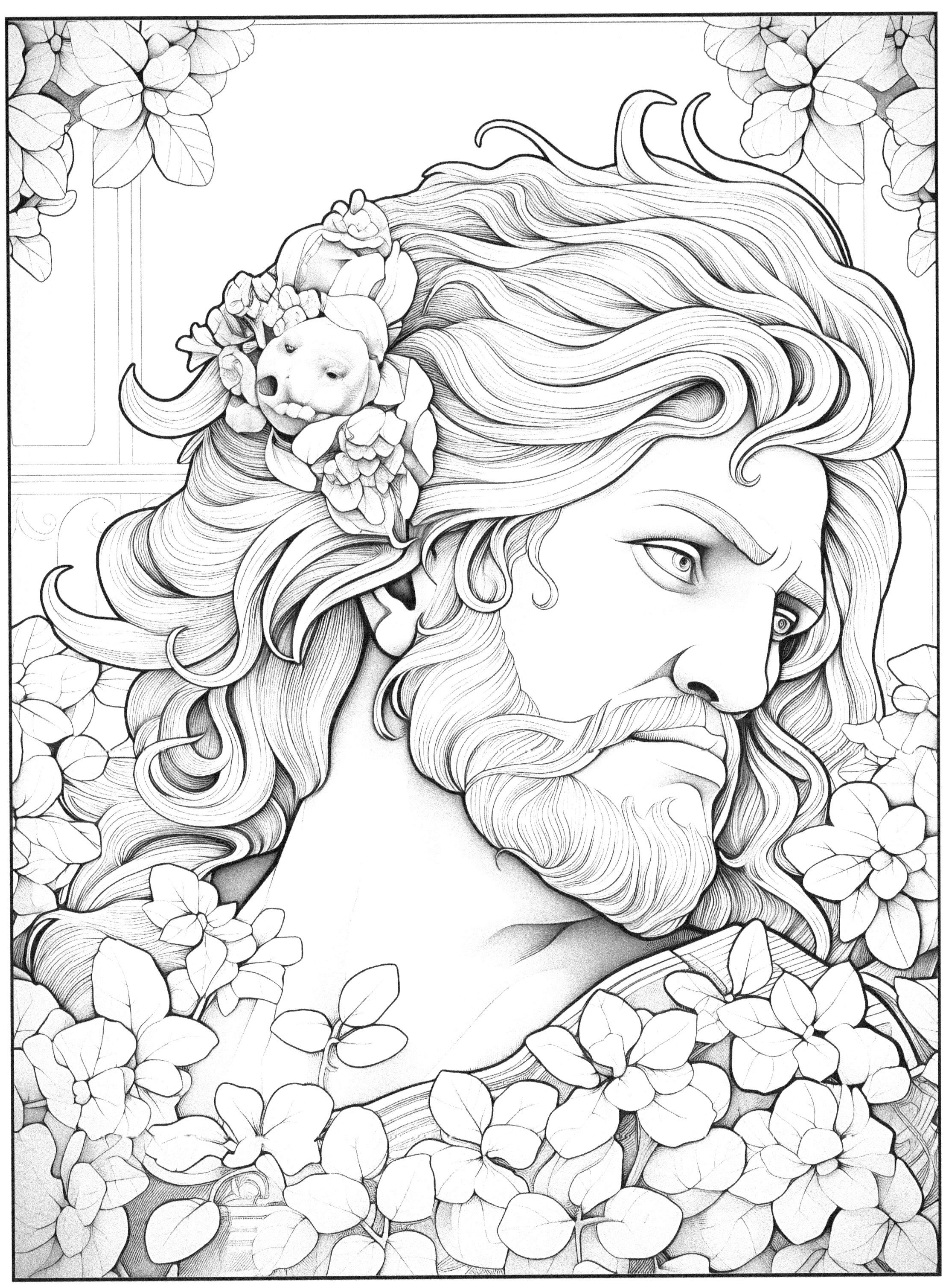

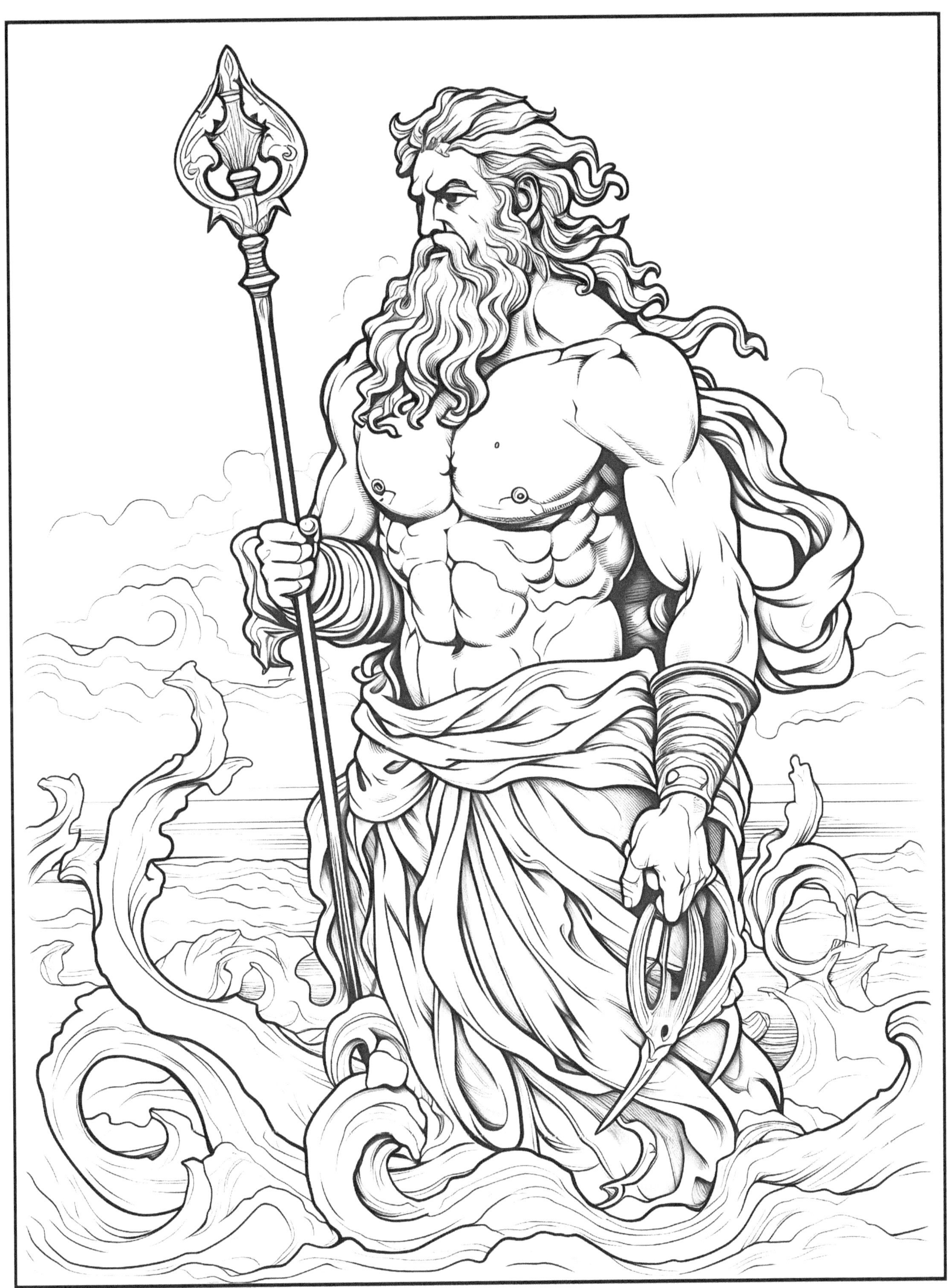

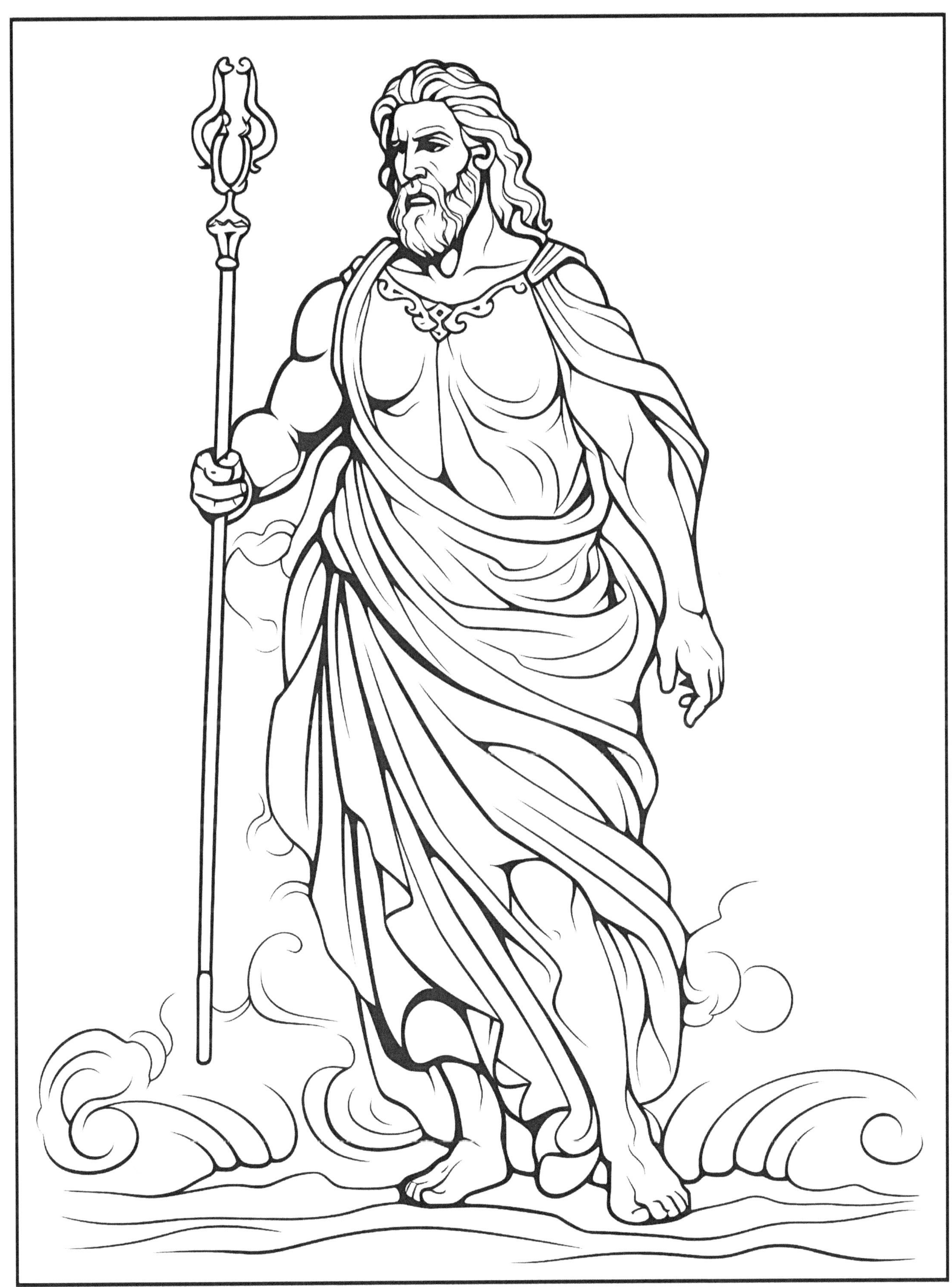

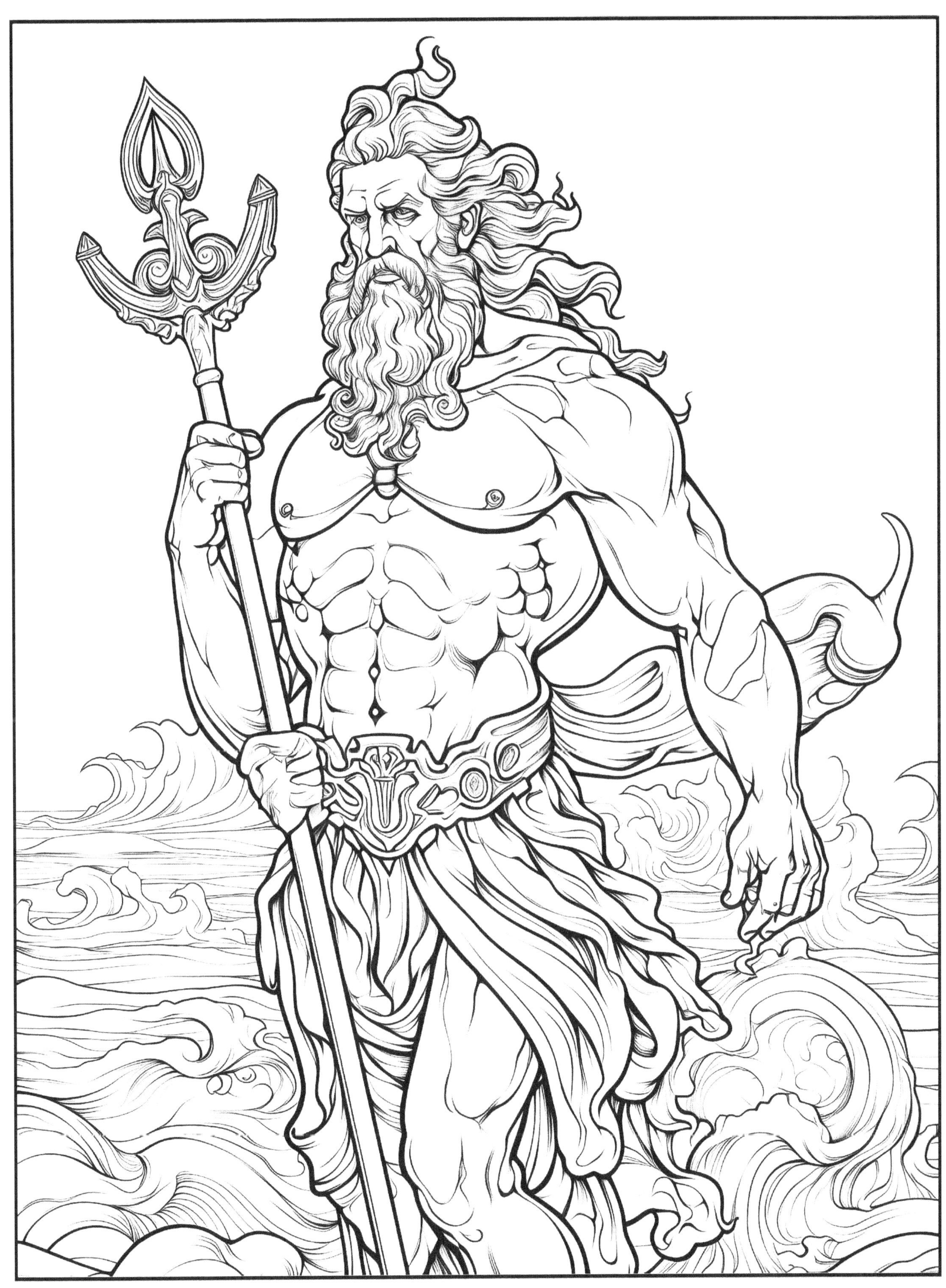

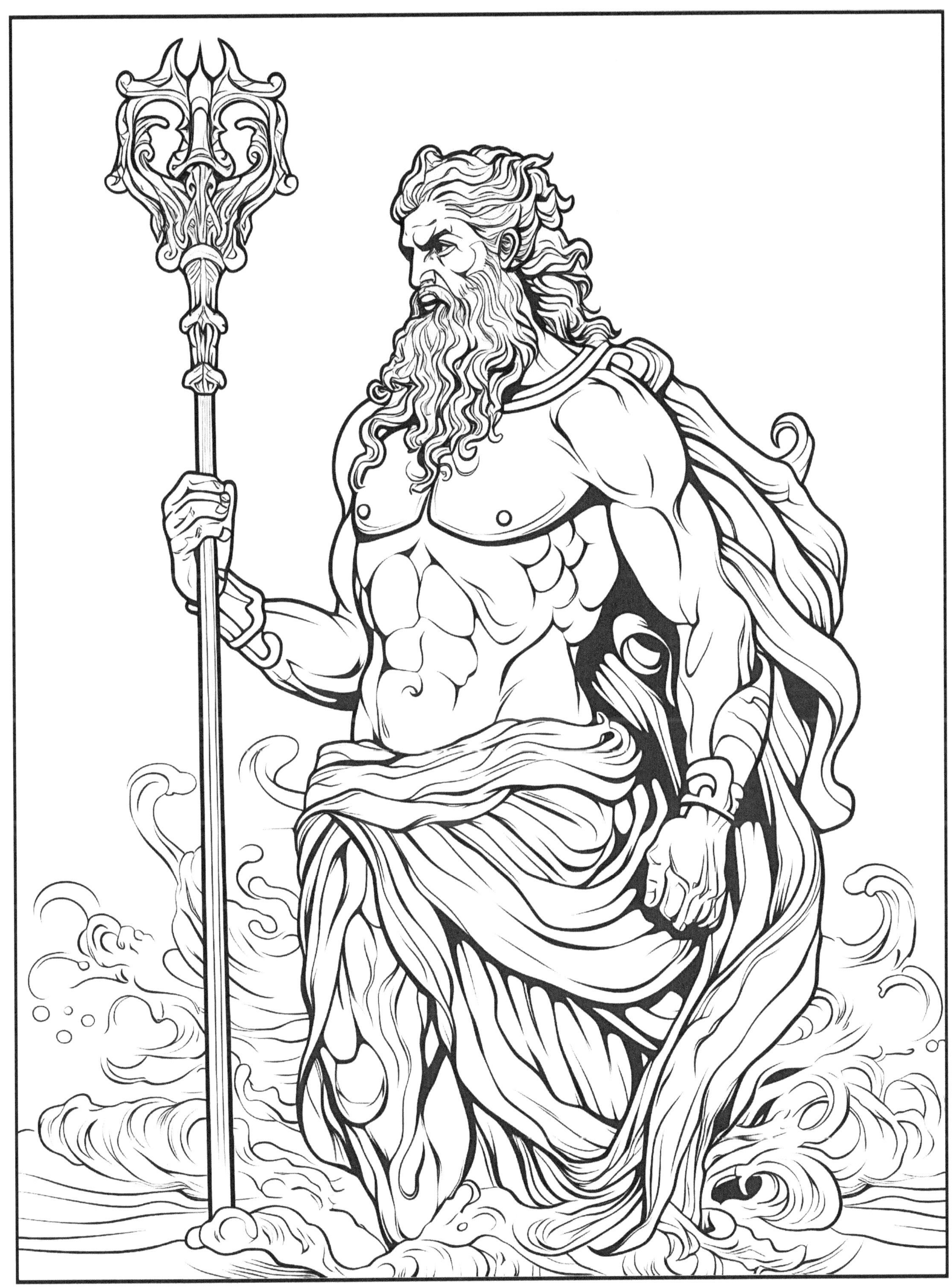

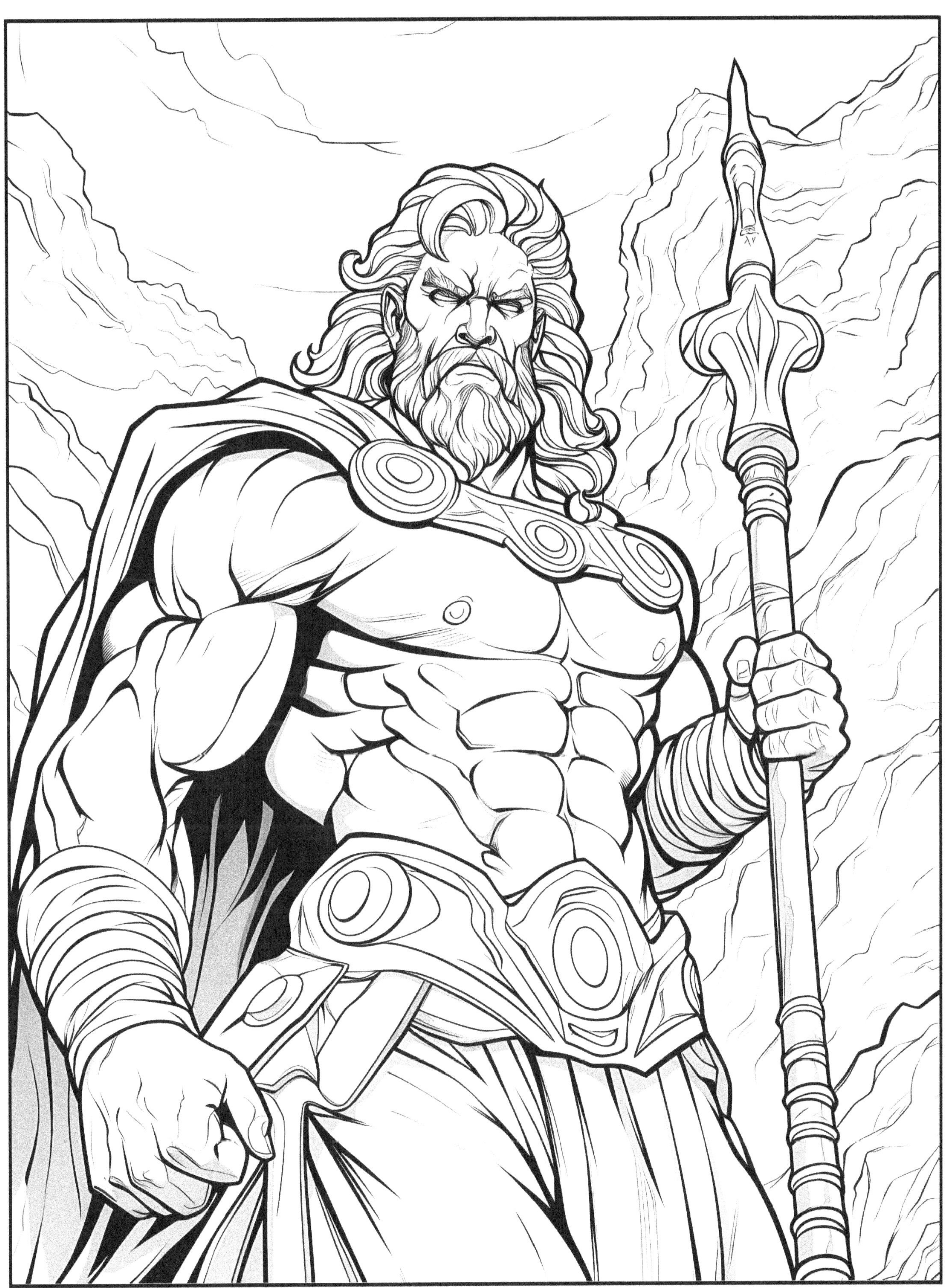

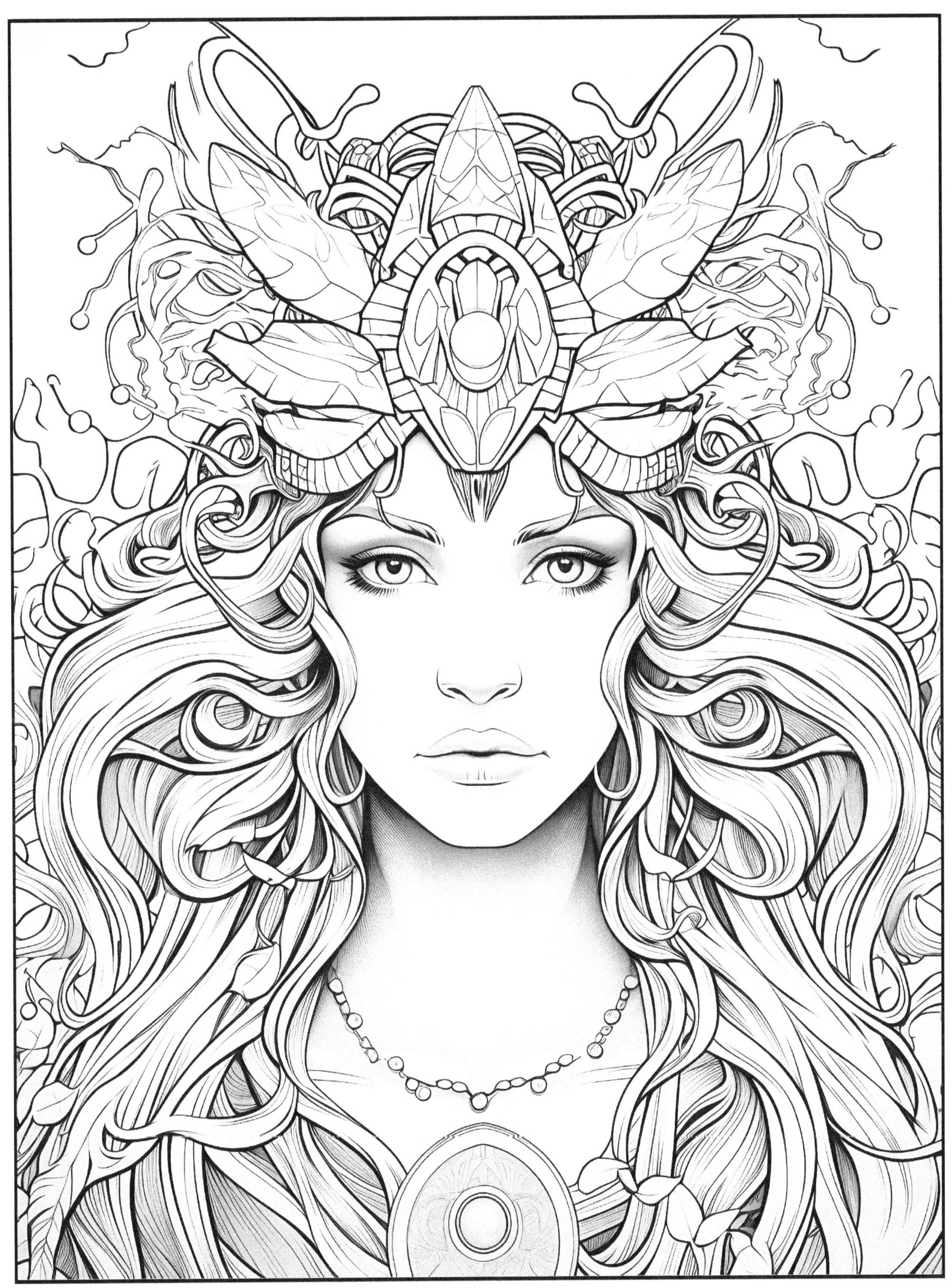

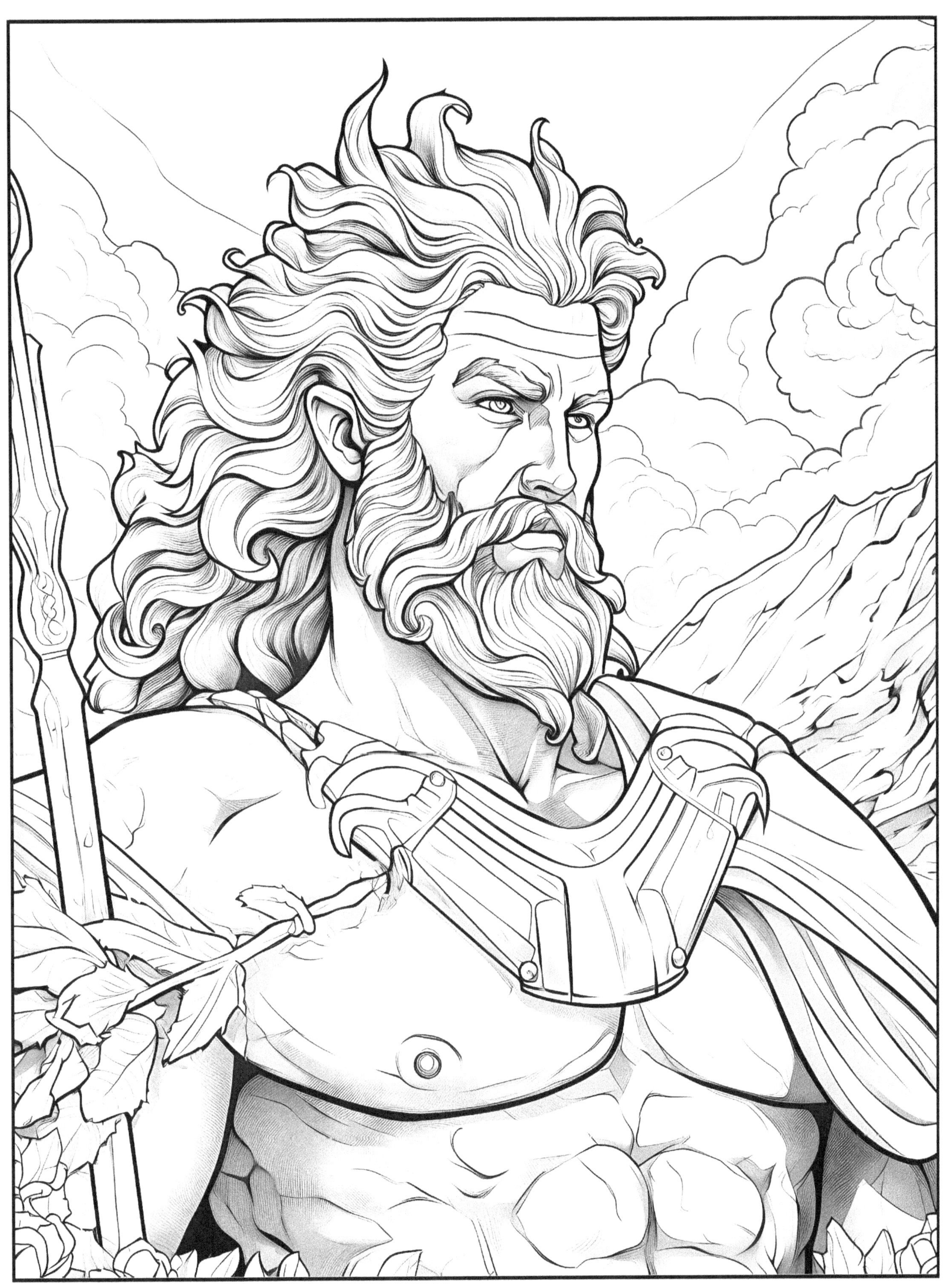

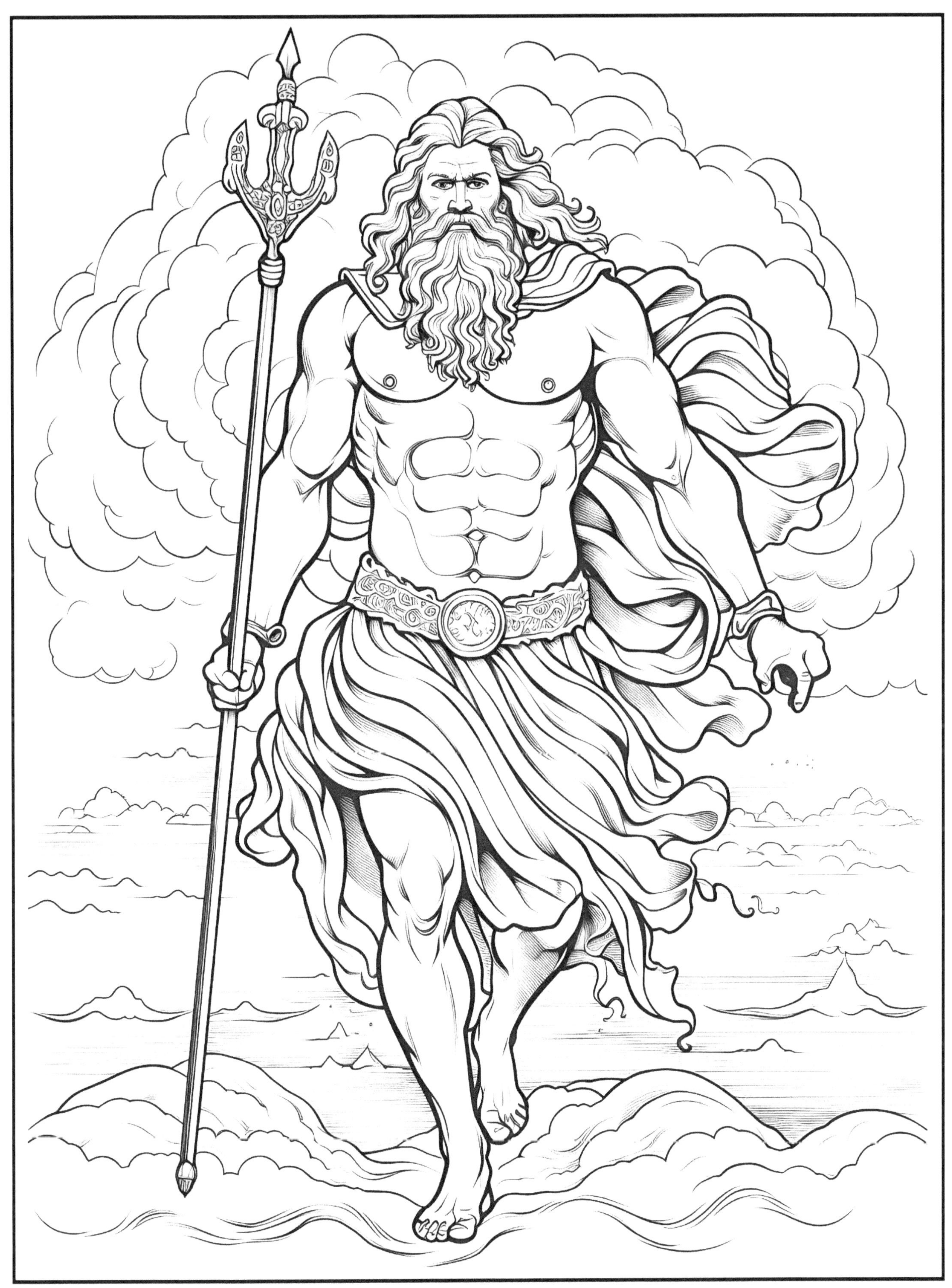

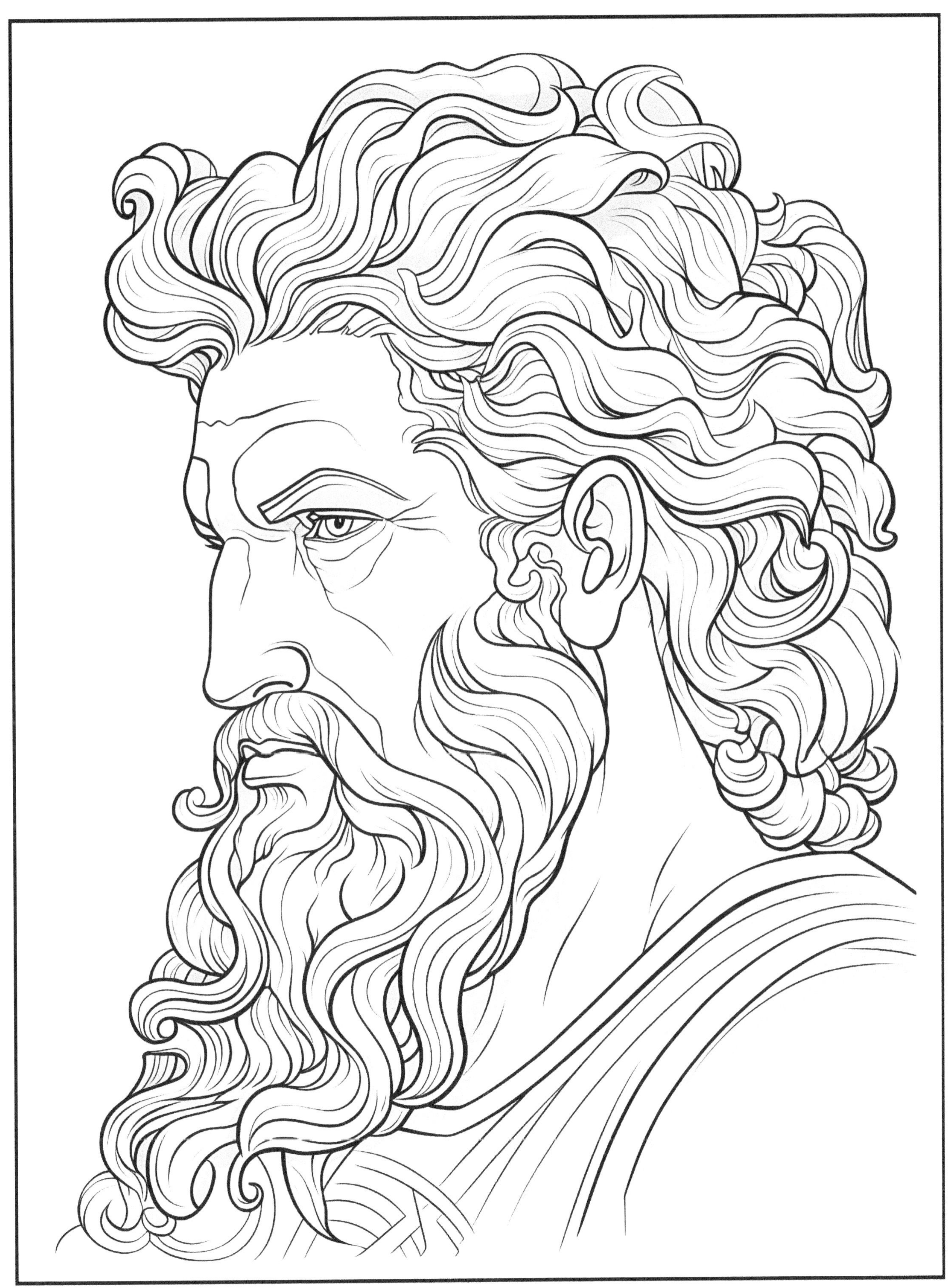

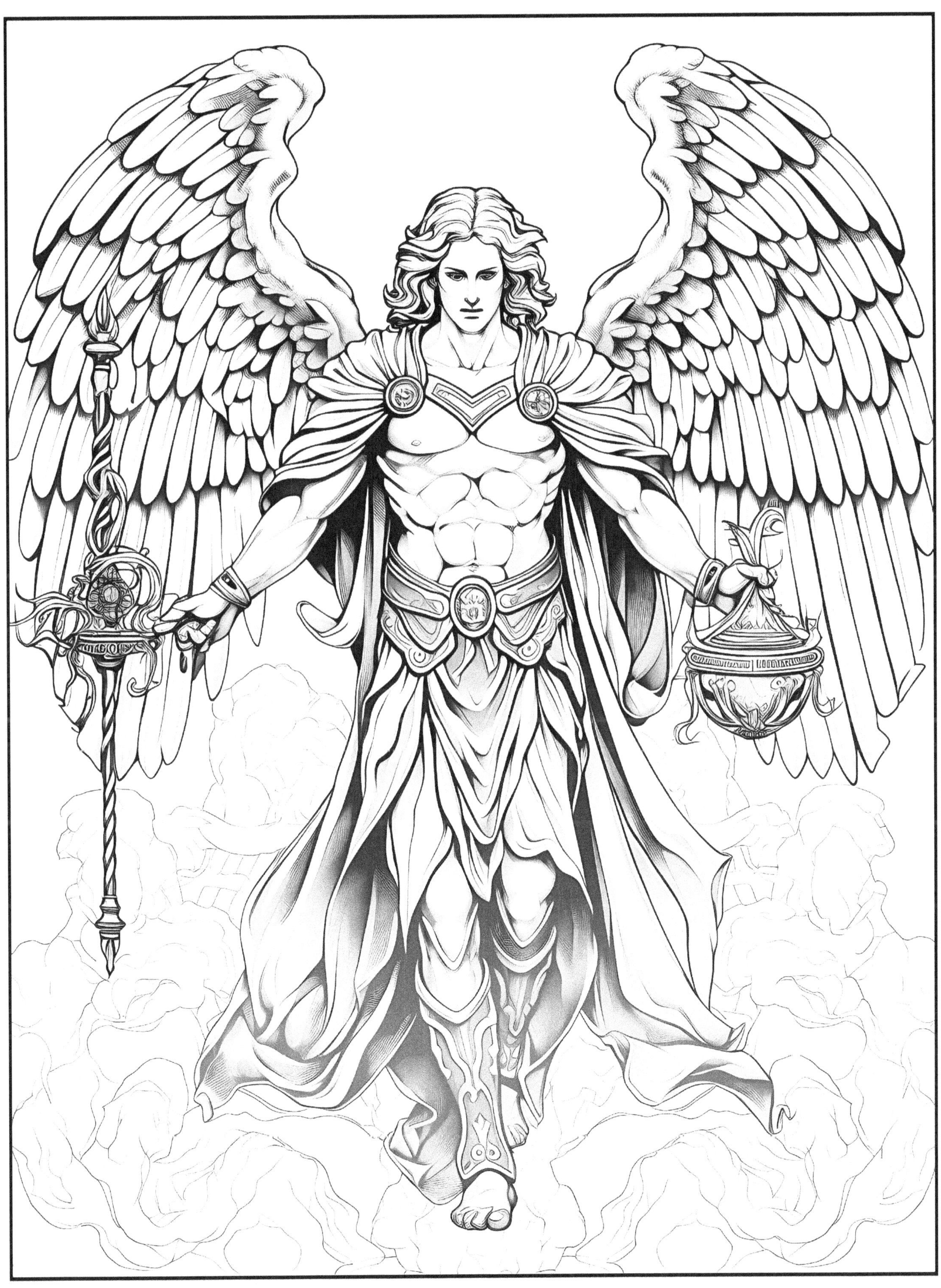

We appreciate you selecting our book, buying our coloring book, and helping our tiny business.

We wish you joy when coloring! We thank all of the contributors to this book for their generosity.

On our Amazon website, kindly post a review and some of your lovely colored photos.

Copyright © 2024 by Al&Vy
All rights reserved

www.ingramcontent.com/pod-product-compliance
Lightning Source LLC
Chambersburg PA
CBHW080222260726
48658CB00008B/2981